Honoring
the Ministry

Honoring the Leaders God
Gives Your Church

MICHAEL D. MILLER

LifeWay Press

Nashville, Tennessee

© Copyright 1998 • LifeWay Press
All rights reserved

ISBN 0-7673-9371-6

Dewey Decimal Classification: 253
Subject Heading: CLERGY-ANNIVERSARIES

PRINTED IN THE UNITED STATES OF AMERICA

All Scripture quotations are from the King James Version of the Bible

LifeWay Christian Resources
of the Southern Baptist Convention
127 Ninth Avenue North
Nashville, Tennessee 37234

Table of **Contents**

Study Guides and Teaching Strategies

written by

Yvonne Burrage

Yvonne is a former elementary school teacher and is presently a homemaker and freelance writer. She has written teaching suggestions for all ages of adult Sunday School curriculum, listening guides for audio sermon series, and study guides to accompany such books as the reprint of *Confronting Casual Christianity* by Dr. Charles Stanley and *Kingdom Principles for Church Growth* by Dr. Gene Mims. Yvonne has just co-authored an interactive study, *God's Call: The Cornerstone of Effective Ministry.*

Introduction

Let the elders that rule well be counted worthy of double honor, especially
they who labour in the word and doctrine. 1 Timothy 5:17.

The church was filled to capacity. There was a sense of anticipation in the crowd. The beloved pastor stood at the pulpit to say thank you for the gifts, kind words, and loving support of the church throughout his ministry. He talked about the joys of the past, especially the accomplishments they had experienced as a church. It was too difficult to thank each member personally for how he or she had ministered to the pastor and his family. There were expressions of joy and of thanks among the congregation. Added to the emotion of the moment was a realization that this is the way God intended for relationships to exist between minister and church.

During my 20-plus years in pastoral ministry, I was blessed to serve in churches with deacons, committees, and individual believers who honored my family and me as their pastor or staff leader. Much of what has happened in my life in leadership is the result of the humbling yet stimulating blessings of honor. *There is no way to judge the power of honor on the life of a leader.* This book is about honor, which in its purest form means recognizing God and others as more significant than yourself. Such honor glorifies God. It is what God intends to exist in the church. God's will is that the church practice "double honor" for the ministers He gives your church.

More than one person's ministry has been extended beyond adversity because of honor received. Expressions of honor come many times from the most unlikely sources. A famous minister tells the story of being sick and unable to preach for an extended period of time in his church. He received a number of letters during his illness. The one that encouraged him most came from a 12-year-old girl who wrote on behalf of herself and her brother. She wrote that she was praying for the preacher's speedy recovery and hoping that he would be back in the pulpit soon. She then gave the reason for her prayer. She wrote, "You are the only preacher we can understand." This little girl honored her preacher with that card of encouragement.

Nothing is more rewarding than kind words spoken in response to one's ministry. "A word fitly spoken is like apples of gold in pictures of silver" (Prov. 25:11).

The subject of honor has not received much attention in the Christian world. No books on honor exist among those on church leadership. A cursory review of any bookstore will confirm that there are few books that deal with biblical honor or the more specific issue of honoring the ministers of the church.

The purpose of this book is to provide the church with understanding of the biblical principles of honor so that appropriate honor will be shown to all the leaders God has given the church.

The book offers deacons, personnel committees, pastor-search committees, and other members of the church valuable ideas about improving the practice of honor for ministers. It challenges those laypersons to consider what their church is doing to become more sensitive to the needs of the God-given ministers. The book includes:

1. *An overview of what the Bible teaches about honor.* This provides the opportunity to look at the scriptural foundations for honor. People may be having trouble honoring their ministers, but they still will believe the Bible.

2. *Explanation of the principle of "double honor" in Scripture.* The concept of double honor is not well known in the church. This section explains what the Bible teaches about this important truth.

3. *Suggestions on how to give double honor in your church.* Practical ideas on how various churches are giving honor to their ministers are included.

We dishonor God when we dishonor our ministers. What is so special about them? God called them and gave them to us. May God give us the grace to see the truth about honor, repent of our disobedience, and honor God by showing double honor to our ministers.

Michael Miller

Chapter 1

The Need for **Honor** in the Church

A son honoreth his father, and a servant his master:
if then I be a father, where is mine honor?
and if I be a master, where is my fear? Malachi 1:6.

Troublesome trends exist in many churches today. The trends remind us that from the beginning, the church has had its problems and conflicts. We need only to turn to the Lord Jesus' words to the churches in the Book of Revelation to recognize that fact.

Church conflicts are as old as the earliest days of the church and yet as contemporary as today's news. Churches and ministers have had their share of good relationships. Most churches have loved their ministers, and God has blessed the ministries of those churches. Other churches have not been as fortunate.

If you have ever belonged to a church involved in conflict with a minister, you know the emotions associated with the situation. Accusations are made about the minister. People in the community talk about the troubles. Members are embarrassed. Erroneous information is communicated. Church leaders are frustrated. Many books have been written on the subject of church conflict, but problems still persist.

It is good to rise above the conflicts and look at what the Bible says about the situation. Perhaps in our attempt to deal with quick solutions we have overlooked something essential in resolving conflicts in the church, notably that most conflicts are over power and control and difficulties in personal relationships between ministers and the church. Conflict between ministers and churches dishonors the church. Ministers' families are hurt. Lifelong scars remain for those caught in these tragic circumstances. Most of all, God is dishonored.

What could God say to the church to help resolve conflicts? Is there an answer to stop the heartache and pain associated with these issues? Does God have a solution that would reduce the conflicts between churches and ministers? Is there an answer that will result in extended tenure in a minister's service to churches? What will restore the blessings of God on the church?

The resolution of those problems will come as the result of a new attitude. The solution to conflict and church problems is practicing the principles of biblical honor. The church needs to return to the basic truths about honor.

A quick examination of a concordance will reveal 190 references to honor in the Bible. The truths about honor are evident throughout Scripture.

As the Old Testament closed, God spoke to His people through the prophet Malachi. Dreadful days were about to come on the nation of Israel. It would be a time when there would not be a word from God—a time of silence. What caused that time to come? Scholars believe that a period of approximately 400 years existed between the close of the Book of Malachi and the Book of Matthew. Malachi declared the situation to Israel. "A son honoreth his father, and a servant his master: if then I be a father, where is mine honor? and if I be a master, where is my fear? saith the Lord of hosts unto you, O priests, that despise my name" (Mal.1:6). Israel had dishonored God. The people had ignored His laws of sacrifice, giving God the worst gift and keeping the best. *God judged a nation for dishonoring Him through their selfish disobedience.*

God asks the church today, "Where is My honor?" Where is God's honor in the conflicts over power in the church? Where is God's honor when a church and its ministers cannot work together? Where is God's honor when we don't give Him our best? God asks "Where is My honor" when there are broken relationships in the church. The church has forgotten what God called us to be. Jesus prayed, "I in them, and thou in me, that they may be made perfect in one; and that the world may know that thou hast sent me, and hast loved them, as thou hast loved me" (John 17:23). Jesus' prayer for the church today is that it will demonstrate the glory of God by unity of purpose and spirit. Church conflicts don't honor God. Individual disobedience in our Christian lives dishonors God. When we do not treat the ministers God has given the church with honor, how can we say that we honor God?

Ask any group of church members what they think about honoring their ministers, and you will get diverse answers. Most people have no idea concerning the nature of honor. Some will say that honoring the minister is no longer necessary in today's society. Another person may say that if you show honor to ministers, it will feed their ego. Someone else may comment that honoring ministers will lead to a separation between members of the church and ministers of the church, especially if ministers do not honor members for their calling in the body of Christ. Another may comment that the only ones who deserve honor as ministers are those who have served God for many years and have earned honor.

Few people in the church seem to understand the importance of giving honor to God, others, and ministers. Even so, the church needs to give honor more today than ever before.

Several factors must be considered when thinking about honor. We obviously should recognize possible misconceptions about honor in the church.

1. *Honor is not relevant today.* Many of those who even think about honor believe that it is a concept that has no relevance in modern society. They believe that giving honor represents an outdated attitude that comes from biblical times.

2. *Honor will lead to pride.* Some believe that to show honor will produce pride in the individual receiving it. They believe that God alone should be honored.

3. *Honor must be earned.* Modern society has established this attitude as the basis for honor. A leader must lead well to receive honor. (See 1 Tim. 5:17.) Today, however, the athletic and entertainment worlds show honor to champions—the biggest, the best, and the brightest.

4. *Honor makes people act superior to others.* Some people think that showing honor creates class systems. If you give honor, then a spirit of superiority will develop. That can create division among Christians.

5. *Honor is favoritism.* Many people today think that showing honor will lead to favoritism. It will communicate the wrong message and highlight certain individuals above others.

6. *Honor is partiality.* For some, honor simply is another method of showing partiality. They believe that it will produce preferences among Christians.

7. *Honor is power.* Some people believe that granting honor to others gives them power that may be used improperly.

Those are just a few of the possible misconceptions about honor that must be recognized as we begin this study of honor. All of them are incorrect. They are misunderstandings of biblical honor.

The church must understand the importance of the kind of honor that impacts our relationship with God, others, and ministers. The Bible clearly reveals the essential elements of honor. The biblical truths serve as the basis of this study. We explore them in detail. At times you are challenged to consider your personal practices of honor. Perhaps some readers will be convicted about what their church should be doing concerning honoring the ministers God has given their church.

What Is Honor?

Honor in the Old Testament

The primary word in the Old Testament for honor can be translated as "weight" or "substance." This reveals that those who are honored are individuals worthy of reverence and respect.

★ Honor is associated with royalty in the Old Testament. It is a word associated with kings. For example, God honored a king in Psalm 21:5: "His glory is great in thy salvation: honor and majesty hast thou laid upon him." In 2 Chronicles 32:27, God honored King Hezekiah: "Hezekiah had exceeding much riches and honor." The story of Esther also illustrates the Old Testament understanding of honor. Esther 6:8 reveals how the king of Persia honored Mordecai the Jew: "Let the royal apparel be brought which the king useth to wear, and the horse that the king rideth upon, and the crown royal which is set upon his head." Then, the king honored Mordecai with a parade: "Bring him on horseback through the street of the city" (Esth. 6:9). The king commanded respect for the faithful man in verse 11: "Thus shall it be done unto the man whom the king delighteth to honor."

★ Honor is associated with persons in positions of authority requiring respect. The individuals were to be honored above others. The Old Testament characterizes honor as the act of giving *recognition, respect,* and *rewards* to those who are in exalted positions. The act of giving honor is expected from those who are placed in submission to such individuals. The Book of Leviticus describes the actions of recognition as related to honor: "Ye shall do no unrighteousness in judgment" (Lev. 19:15). Respect is described in Deuteronomy 5:16: "Honor thy father and thy mother, as the Lord thy God hath commanded thee." God rewarded Solomon in an unexpected way: "I have also given thee that which thou hast not asked, both riches, and honor" (1 Kings 3:13; also see 2 Chron. 1:11-12.).

★ Honor in the Old Testament is connected to obedience to God. When honor is given to those who are worthy to receive it, obedience is also given to God. One's obedience to God can be judged based on honor given to those individuals whom God has placed in positions of authority over the person.

★ Honoring God by living in obedience to His laws and instructions is a key principle in the Old Testament. Honor begins with obeying God. Following honor to God is honor of those in positions of authority. When honor is given to such individuals, honor is given to God.

Honor in the New Testament

The New Testament word for honor can be translated "reverence," "esteem," "dignity," "recognition," "value," or "respect." The word implies elevation—lifting an individual to a position of superiority.

The New Testament describes honor as praise. The term implies qualities in an individual that reflect excellence and godliness.

★ Honor in the New Testament is given to those in positions of *authority.* Several different kinds of positions of authority are mentioned in the New Testament. These positions of authority include government officials, employers, leaders in the church, and parents. Peter said, "Honor the king" (1 Pet. 2:17). Paul called on Christians to "be subject unto the higher powers [government authorities]" (Rom. 13:1) and commanded, "Honor thy father and mother; which is the first commandment with promise" (Eph. 6:2).

★ Honor in the New Testament is associated with *relationships.* It speaks of honor in relationships between individuals and emphasizes both the importance of relationships and the living of holy lives.

★ Honor in the New Testament is to be shown to those having special relationships. In the New Testament, special relationships require honor—marriage relationships, relationships in the church between members, and care for widows. "Be kindly affectioned one to another with brotherly love; in honor preferring one another" (Rom. 12:10); "Honor widows that are widows indeed" (1 Tim. 5:3); "Husbands, dwell with them according to knowledge, giving honor unto the wife, as unto the weaker vessel, and as being heirs together of the grace of life" (1 Pet. 3:7); "Let every one of you in particular so love his wife even as himself; and the wife see that she reverence her husband" (Eph. 5:33).

★ Honor in the New Testament is to be given to all people. It is to go to those who are a part of the family of God and also to those who are not in the church.

★ Honor will be obvious at the judgment seat of Christ. (See 2 Cor. 5:10.) The judgment seat of Christ is a place where either honor or dishonor will be given. It will be at the point in time when God will bring His people to accountability, when He will commend and honor His people for their works in the flesh on earth. It will also be a time when dishonor will be given to those who have not lived for the Lord.

★ Honor will be the focus of heaven. The Book of Revelation directs all honor back to God and the Lamb. We see the elders casting down their crowns before the throne, the creatures and saints of heaven singing and honoring the Lamb of God, and the nations and kings of the world bringing honor before God. The final book of the Bible expresses that *all honor belongs to the Triune God.*

★ Honoring God is seen in the New Testament when it is given to the Son of God, Jesus Christ. When we honor Jesus Christ as Savior and Lord and when we serve Him, we show honor to God. Those who dishonor the Savior dishonor God.

The significance of honor in Scripture should not be overlooked or ignored. Honor requires that respect, recognition, and rewards be given to those whom God has deemed worthy of honor.

The giving of honor is practiced in the context of relationships. It is demonstrated through submission and obedience to those who are called to places of authority and responsibility. Honor for God is the basis of all honor. Obedience to God is coupled to the honor we give to God.

Biblical Principles of Honor

1. All honor belongs to Jesus Christ.

2. God honors those who honor Him.

3. When we surrender to the lordship of Jesus Christ, we honor God.

4. When we worship in spirit and truth, we honor God.

5. When we give our possessions to God, we honor God.

6. When we honor each other, we honor God.

7. When we submit to authorities, we honor God.

8. When we give double honor to ministers, we honor God.

God asks the church, "Where is My honor?" What is your answer to God? The church must return to God with a renewed commitment to honor Him in all our relationships. We must return to God and reverently honor Him as Lord and glorify His name. As the church honors God in these ways, He is glorified among the nations.

Study Guide

1. Describe how your church honors the following people:
    a. Staff members _____
    b. Deacons _____
    c. Sunday School workers _____
    d. Older, faithful church members _____

2. What misconceptions do you think your church has regarding giving honor to those in ministry?_____

_____

_____

3. Explain what kinds of individuals were honored in the Old Testament.

_____

_____

4. In what ways is honor connected to God in the Old Testament? _____

_____

5. Define in your own words the meaning of New Testament honor._____

_____

6. Dr. Miller discusses seven examples of honor being given in the New Testament.
Briefly describe each type of honor given:
- Honor given to those in positions of a _____
- Honor associated with r_____
- Honor given in special r _____
- Honor given to all p_____
- Honor directed in heaven toward G _____
- Honoring God when honoring the S_____

7. In light of the honor given in the New Testament, how would you answer God today if He asked you personally, "Where is My Honor?"

_____

_____

_____

8. How would relationships in your church—your personal life—change if the biblical principles of honor were followed? _____

_____

_____

9. Turn in your book to page 12 and circle three principles which you need to commit to God in your own life.

10. List the three principles you circled, and identify ways you will put honor into practice.

     Principle _____

     Practice: _____

     Principle: _____

     Practice: _____

     Principle: _____

     Practice: _____

What Would You Do? A group of charter members in your church is thinking of leaving the congregation because they feel they are no longer needed. One of the first deacons of the church said, "Our group is not considered a part of this church; we are overlooked, neglected, and ignored." As a lay leader in your church, what would you do to remedy this situation? What steps do you think the church should take to restore these older members to the body?

Chapter 2

Honoring God

Them that honor me I will honor, and they that despise
me shall be lightly esteemed. 1 Samuel 2:30

The times were dark and difficult in Israel. The sons of Eli, the high priest, had made a mockery of the spiritual work of the priesthood. "Now the sons of Eli were sons of Belial; they knew not the Lord" (1 Sam. 2:12). These two worthless men did not serve God appropriately and were not obedient to Him in their spiritual leadership over Israel. They were also disobedient to God's Word regarding the sacrifices of the people to God detailed in Leviticus 3:3-5. "Wherefore the sin of the young men was very great before the Lord: for men abhorred the offering of the Lord" (1 Sam. 2:17).

The sons of Eli dishonored God by their immoral living. Their father knew of their wickedness. "Now Eli was very old, and heard all that his sons did unto all Israel; and how they lay with the women that assembled at the door of the tabernacle of the congregation" (1 Sam. 2:22). Though Eli confronted his sons about their behavior, they would not listen. Their sin as leaders led the people to sin and dishonor God. "Nay, my sons; for it is no good report that I hear: ye make the Lord's people to transgress" (1 Sam. 2:24).

An unnamed prophet ("man of God," KJV) came to Eli. He reminded Eli that it was God who had revealed Himself to Eli's father in Egypt. "Did I plainly appear unto the house of thy father, when they were in Egypt in Pharaoh's house?" (1 Sam. 2:27).

The man told Eli that God had chosen his father and his household to be the spiritual leaders of Israel. "Did I choose him out of all the tribes of Israel to be my priest, to offer upon mine altar, to burn incense, to wear an ephod before me?" (1 Sam. 2:28). God had chosen the tribe of Aaron to be His priests for the nation of Israel. God honored them as His chosen tribe.

The man further declared to Eli, "And did I give unto the house of thy father all the offerings made by fire of the children of Israel?" (1 Sam. 2:28). God had provided the priests with food through the offerings brought by the people. He honored them by providing for their needs even after the priests had taken advantage of the people (vv.13-16).

Then the prophet of God made clear to Eli his great sin. "Wherefore kick ye at my sacrifice and at mine offering, which I have commanded in my habitation; and honorest thy sons above me, to make yourselves fat with the chiefest of all the offerings of Israel my people?" (1 Sam. 2:29). Eli was guilty of *honoring his sons more than God.* He neglected to honor God with the best of the offerings, taking it for himself and his family rather than giving it to God. He dishonored God by placing his family and his personal wants before God.

The unnamed prophet then predicted God's response of judgment to such actions. "Wherefore the Lord God of Israel saith, . . . for them that honor me I will honor, and they that despise me shall be lightly esteemed" (1 Sam. 2:30).

God's Eternal Principle of Honor

The story of Eli and his two sons illustrates God's eternal principle of honor. The Bible says that God is worthy of honor and obedience. When honor and obedience are given to God, they are given back by God. This principle is a spiritual law of God, immutable much like the natural laws of the universe. This principle is illustrated throughout Scripture. Therefore, honoring God is the responsibility of every believer. Obedience to God's Word and ways expresses honor to God. As a result, God responds to our obedience by honoring us. The scriptural principle is clear: *Honor God, and He will Honor you; dishonor God, and He will dishonor you.*

We, much like Israel, have neglected to honor God. "A son honoreth his father, and a servant his master: if then I be a father, where is mine honor? and if I be a master, where is my fear? saith the Lord of hosts unto you, O priests, that despise my name. And ye say, Wherein what way have we despised thy name? . . . And if ye offer the blind for sacrifice, is it not evil? and if ye offer the lame and sick, is it not evil? offer it now unto thy governor; will he be pleased with thee, or accept thy person? saith the Lord of hosts. . . . I have no pleasure in you" (Mal. 1:6,8,10).

What Jesus said of His generation is still true today: "Ye hypocrites, well did Esaias prophesy of you, saying, This people draweth nigh unto me with their mouth, and honoreth me with their lips; but their heart is far from me" (Matt. 15:7-8). If we honor God only with our lips and our actions do not conform to His word, we are living as hypocrites.

The world honors people by recognizing the biggest, the best, and the brightest. Homes and offices proudly display trophies and certificates of achievement. But in the context of the kingdom of God, honor takes on an entirely different focus. True honor is a matter of the heart, not the mind. Honor is grounded in submission and obedience to God.

The selfish people of Israel dishonored God by their disobedience to His commands. The hypocritical people of Jesus' day honored God with their lips but were not willing to honor Him with their hearts. Today, many dishonor God in both of those ways.

Honoring God is foundational to our relationship with God. Understanding and giving honor is crucial for every believer's spiritual growth and development. Honoring God demonstrates our obedience to God. Honoring God shows our reverence for God. Honoring God is the response of a redeemed and grateful believer. Regrettably, like Eli and his sons, people today dishonor God in their lives and relationships. Ministries are damaged because people do not treat God-called church leaders with the honor due them. The glory has departed from many churches because God has not been honored by them.

Eli and his sons dishonored God by:

1. Taking what belonged to God and keeping it for themselves.

2. Living in immorality and open rebellion toward God.

3. Neglecting their God-given ministries to lead God's chosen people to honor Him through worship and stewardship.

The man of God prophesied to Eli that God's judgment would come on him and his family because they had dishonored God's name in their priestly service (1 Sam. 2: 31-36). Those judgments were:

1. Eli's family would be cut off (vv. 31-33).

2. Eli's sons would die on the same day (v. 34).

3. Eli's family would be reduced to poverty (v. 36).

4. Eli's family would never again serve in the priesthood (v. 36).

God dishonored Eli and his sons. We read in 1 Samuel 4 that God harshly judged Eli and Israel because of the sins of Eli and his sons. "And the Philistines fought, and Israel was smitten, and they fled every man to his tent: and there was a very great slaughter; for there fell of Israel thirty thousand footmen. And the ark of God was taken; and the two sons of Eli, Hophni and Phinehas, were slain. . . . And it came to pass, . . . that he fell from off the seat backward by the side of the gate, and his neck brake, and he died: . . . And she said, The glory is departed from Israel: for the ark of God is taken" (1 Sam. 4:10-11,18,22).

God's judgment came on Israel because of the sin of dishonoring God through disobedience. The ark of the covenant was captured, Israel's high priest died, and God's glory and blessing departed from Israel. The words of the man of God to Eli were prophetic: "Them that honor me I will honor, and they that despise me shall be lightly esteemed" (1 Sam. 2:30).

What does it mean to honor God? We see that Scripture is clear regarding the believer's responsibility to honor God. So, as we consider the subject of honor, we begin with a review of what the Bible says about honoring God. Honoring God is an important biblical principle. Until we Christians honor God, we will fail to honor the ministers God gives us.

We Honor God Through Discipleship

Honoring God makes us like Jesus. Jesus honored God the Father with His whole life. He said, "I honor my Father" (John 8:49). His life was an expression of honor for God. He set the example for all believers. He sought to do only those things that would please God. Jesus lived His life on earth as an expression of honor to God. The same should be true of His followers. Believers are like Jesus Christ when they honor God.

When Jesus was in the world, He called people to follow Him. The Book of John records that Jesus found Philip in Galilee and said, "Follow me" (John 1:43). Even today Jesus Christ calls people to a life of discipleship. "Whosoever will come after me, let him deny himself, and take up his cross, and follow me" (Mark 8:34). Honoring God begins with a commitment to follow Jesus for life. This sometimes is called the life of obedience, or discipleship, the first of three great principles regarding honoring God. The word *disciple* means follower.

Honoring God begins as we recognize that Jesus Christ is worthy of all honor. We must honor Jesus, not ourselves. A life of honor is a life of surrender to Him. The Bible makes clear what we must do to begin a life of following Jesus: "If thou shalt confess with thy mouth the Lord Jesus, and shalt believe in thine heart that God hath raised him from the dead, thou shalt be saved. For with the heart man believeth unto righteousness; and with the mouth confession is made unto salvation" (Rom. 10:9-10).

The Jews questioned the honor of Jesus after He had healed a man at the pool of Bethesda. Jesus had healed the man on the Sabbath. The religious leaders could not understand how Jesus could do such a thing on the Sabbath. It appeared to them to be a lack of honor toward God. Jesus discussed with them in John 5 His relationship with God the Father. The Jewish leaders refused to listen to Jesus' explanation of His relationship with the Father. He then reminded the leaders of His work and its relationship to the work of God. "My Father worketh hitherto, and I work" (John 5:17). The leaders then sought to kill him for they understood but rejected his statement that he was equal with God the Father. Because Jesus Christ is fully God, He deserves honor. He alone has the honor of being the Son of God.

Jesus, knowing that the Jewish religious leaders had rejected Him and refused to acknowledge Him as Lord, said, "For the Father judgeth no man, but hath committed all judgment unto the Son: That all men should honor the Son, even as they honor the Father. He that honoreth not the Son honoreth not the Father which hath sent him" (John 5:22-23).

Here Jesus identified the first great principle of honoring God. Honoring God begins when we honor Jesus Christ and submit to Him as Savior and Lord.

When we don't honor Jesus Christ, we don't honor God. We are to honor the Lord Jesus Christ as One having all authority and judgment. "Verily, verily, I say unto you, He that heareth my word, and believeth on him that sent me, hath everlasting life, and shall not come into condemnation; but is passed from death unto life" (John 5:24). Honoring God is expressed in a life surrendered to the Lord Jesus Christ, that is, by being a disciple.

In Jesus' discussion with the Pharisees, He based His honor on His *authority*. When He had healed the man by the pool of Bethesda, He demonstrated His authority over sickness. Jesus Christ holds all authority over sickness and works even on the Sabbath. We who recognize that fact call on the Lord to heal the sick. Jesus Christ is the Great Physician. Throughout His earthly ministry He healed the sick through His singular authority and power, and He continues to do so today.

Jesus' honor was based on His having the authority to do the work of God as the Christ, the Son of God. The Jews understood that fact and tried to kill Him. (See John 5:18.) As the Son of God Jesus does what the Father does. Jesus said, "Verily, verily, I say unto you, The Son can do nothing of himself, but what he seeth the Father do: for what things soever he doeth, these also doeth the Son likewise" (John 5:19). The Father revealed all things to him. "For the Father loveth the Son, and sheweth him all things that himself doeth: and he will shew him greater works than these, that ye may marvel" (John 5:20). Just as the Father raises men from the dead, so does Jesus Christ. He has the power to raise the dead. "For as the Father raiseth up the dead, and quickeneth them; even so the

Son quickeneth whom he will" (John 5:21). He has authority over death. When Jesus raised Lazarus from the dead, His honor was demonstrated to all who saw it. The miracle confirmed that He was the Son of God with authority to raise the dead.

God the Father has committed all judgment to the Son of God. "For the Father judgeth no man, but hath committed all judgment unto the Son" (John 5:22). He has all authority to judge all people and their deeds. The Bible says that there will be a time when believers will stand before the judgment seat of Christ. "For we must all appear before the judgment seat of Christ; that every one may receive the things done in his body, according to that he hath done, whether it be good or bad" (2 Cor. 5:10).

Jesus Christ is to be honored because he has received all authority over sickness, death, and judgment. He is to be honored as Lord of all and over all. Jesus Christ is to receive honor and praise because He is worthy.

Jesus received honor from God the Father. "If I honor myself, my honor is nothing: it is my Father that honoreth me" (John 8:54). The Father honored Jesus Christ by placing all authority and judgment in His care. Paul reminded us: "Wherefore God also hath highly exalted him, and given him a name which is above every name: That at the name of Jesus every knee should bow, of things in heaven, and things in earth, and things under the earth; And that every tongue should confess that Jesus Christ is Lord, to the glory of God the Father" (Phil. 2:9-11).

A life of discipleship honors Jesus Christ. If we follow Christ in a life of discipleship, we will obey His commands. Jesus said, "If ye love me, keep my commandments" (John 14:15). As disciples, we demonstrate our love for God and His Son with a voluntary submission of our will and life because of who God is and what He has done for us.

Avery Willis, author of *MasterLife (MasterLife*, Part 1, © Copyright 1980, 1982 The Sunday School Board of the Southern Baptist Convention, p.8), has given the following outline of the essential characteristics for a life of discipleship:

Discipleship involves a *lifelong commitment to spend time with Jesus Christ*. The importance of a relationship with Jesus Christ is at the heart of discipleship. The first disciples spent time with Jesus throughout His earthly ministry. When Jesus told the crowds the true cost of following Him, many stopped following Him. (See John 6:66.) Jesus then turned to the twelve disciples and asked, "Will ye also go away?" (John 6:67). Peter expressed the principle of discipleship when he said, "Lord, to whom shall we go? thou hast the words of eternal life" (John 6:68). We honor Jesus Christ when we accept Him as Savior and Lord of our lives and become His disciples.

A life of discipleship includes *daily time in the Word of God.* Reading, studying, and memorizing Scripture honor Jesus Christ as Lord. God has given the Bible to provide believers with His counsel. When believers study the Scriptures, they are best able to determine God's purposes for their lives. They are able to hear God's counsel concerning the way in which to conduct themselves. Paul reminded Timothy, "All scripture is given by inspiration of God, and is profitable for doctrine, for reproof, for correction, for instruction in righteousness: That the man of God may be perfect, thoroughly furnished unto all good works" (2 Tim. 3:16-17). Jesus frequently referred to the Word of God. He said, "Man shall not live by bread alone, but by every word that proceedeth out of the mouth of God" (Matt. 4:4).

When believers spend time daily in the Scriptures, they are establishing the essential characteristic of a disciple.

A life of discipleship includes *praying in faith.* Jesus said, "And whatsoever ye shall ask in my name, that will I do, that the Father may be glorified in the Son" (John 14:13). We honor Jesus Christ as we pray in faith, believing that the Lord hears our prayers.

A life of discipleship includes *fellowship with believers.* Jesus prayed, "That they all may be one; as thou, Father, art in me, and I in thee, that they also may be one in us: that the world may believe that thou hast sent me" (John 17:21). We honor Jesus Christ when we fellowship with other believers. The importance of the church in the life of the believer cannot be neglected. We honor the Lord when we attend the services and activities of the church.

A life of discipleship calls us to be *witnesses in the world.* Jesus said, "Go ye therefore, and teach all nations, baptizing them in the name of the Father, and of the Son, and of the Holy Ghost" (Matt. 28:19). Jesus is honored as we witness to others about the wonderful love and grace of the Lord Jesus Christ.

A life of discipleship is expressed as we *minister to others.* Jesus said, "Even as the Son of man came not to be ministered unto, but to minister, and to give his life a ransom for many" (Matt. 20:28). Jesus gave His disciples an example of serving others. We honor Jesus when we pattern our life after His.

Following Jesus honors God.—The first mark of honoring God is exhibiting Christlikeness in our lives. Our lives are transformed as we follow Jesus Christ in a life of discipleship. Our honor for Him is then expressed through our lives, not just with our lips. There is no more appropriate way to honor Jesus Christ than by living our lives like Him.

Submission is an act of honor.—Until we surrender the control of our lives to Jesus Christ, we cannot honor God. The essence of true honor is found in the submission of our life to Jesus Christ.

In the ancient Greek games, the umpire would sit on a raised platform. The victorious athletes would stand before him and receive their laurel crowns. That scene describes what it will be like for believers when standing before the judgment seat of Jesus Christ. It will be a *day of honor.* We sometimes focus only on the portion of 2 Corinthians 5:10 that says we will receive judgment from the Lord for the bad we have done in our lives. The verse declares also that judgment will be a time when the Lord honors believers for the good they have done.

Believers honor the Son of God because all authority and all judgment are His. He is worthy of the complete surrender of our life and our submission to His will.

Crowns of Honor

A crown in the Bible is a head wreath given as a prize to the victor in athletic games. It was given also to a person the public wanted to honor It was worn in religious and public ceremonies. The crown in biblical times was a mark of honor or reward.

God honors those who honor Him. He is a God who honors people who submit to Jesus Christ as their Lord. Four crowns are mentioned in the New Testament. They are tokens of honor, that is, recognition for faithful service to Jesus Christ. Biblical honor is expressed by recognition and rewards. The four crowns remind us that when we stand before the Lord, it will be a time of honor and reward for believers who have been faithful to the Lord. Heaven will be a place of honor—a place of reward for good work. When God honors His people, He recognizes them and rewards them. What a joy it will be for God's people and His faithful ministers to hear the Lord say, "Well done, thou good and faithful servant: thou hast been faithful over a few things, I will make thee ruler over many things: enter thou into the joy of thy lord" (Matt. 25:21). Here are the four crowns that the Lord someday will give in honor of those who have honored Him.

The crown of the martyr.—James 1:12 says, "Blessed is the man that endureth temptation: for when he is tried, he shall receive the crown of life, which the Lord hath promised to them that love him." James teaches that those who endure the testing of faith receive reward. The believer who is victorious in his struggle against trials will be rewarded by God.

That does not mean eternal life. Believers have received that already. It does, however, promise a reward of life in eternity that is abundant and beyond compare. In Revelation 2:10 Jesus said to the persecuted church of Smyrna, "Fear none of those things which thou shalt suffer: behold, the devil shall cast some of you into prison, that ye may be tried; and ye shall have tribulation ten days: be thou faithful until death, and I will give thee a crown of life."

The crown of the righteousness.—Second Timothy 4:8 says, "Henceforth there is laid up for me a crown of righteousness, which the Lord, the righteous judge, shall give me at that day: and not to me only, but unto all them also that love his appearing." In Paul's final testimony he wrote that a crown of righteousness is rewarded by the Lord to believers at the end of their lives. His description pictures the crown rewarded to the marathon runner at the end of the race. This reward awaits every believer who runs the Christian race successfully to the finish, waiting for the long-anticipated appearing of the Lord.

The crown of the victor.—First Corinthians 9: 24-27 says, "Know ye not that they which run in a race run all, but one receiveth the prize? So run, that ye may obtain. And every man that striveth for the mastery is temperate in all things. Now they do it to obtain a corruptible crown; but we an incorruptible. I therefore so run, not as uncertainly; so fight I, not as one that beateth the air: But I keep under my body, and bring it into subjection: lest that by any means, when I have preached to others, I myself should be a castaway." Paul wrote to the Corinthian church to remind them that they should be in submission to each other in order to please God. He reminded them that like the athletes of the Greek games, believers should run with all-out effort to win the prize. The crown of the victor is eternal life and fellowship with God that will last forever.

The crown of the minister.—First Peter 5:1-4 says, "The elders which are among you I exhort, who am also an elder, and a witness of the sufferings of Christ, and also a partaker of the glory that shall be revealed: Feed the flock of God which is among you, taking the oversight thereof, not by constraint, but willingly; not for filthy lucre, but of a ready mind; Neither as being lords over God's heritage, but being ensamples to the flock. And when the chief Shepherd shall appear, ye shall receive a crown of glory that fadeth not away." For their faithfulness, ministers will receive a crown of glory that does not fade away. It is not a crown like those rewarded in athletic games that withers and finally is destroyed. Ministers will receive an eternal reward of honor for the work they have done for the Lord.

Believers may not receive many rewards or much recognition in this world, but the day is coming when God will honor His people for their faithfulness to Him. Honoring God begins with completely surrendering our lives to Jesus Christ as Savior and Lord, with the confident expectation of being honored by God. Jesus said, "If any man serve me, let him follow me; and where I am, there shall also my servant be: if any man serve me, him will my Father honor" (John 12:26).

We Honor God through Worship

This is the second great principle. Honoring God is expressed in worship of God. Our English word *worship* comes from the root word "worthship." Worship is expressing our praise for God's worthiness.

Honor is reverencing God in worship. The word *reverence* in the Old Testament can be translated "tremble" or to "bow down." The term implies bowing before one who is superior. Reverence is the basis of honor. Reverence for God must be maintained. "God is greatly to be feared in the assembly of the saints, and to be had in reverence of all them that are about him" (Ps. 89:7). In both heaven and in the church, reverence for God characterizes honor for God.

We Worship God's Character

When the ark of God was brought to Jerusalem and placed in the tabernacle, David praised and worshiped God. He called on Israel to worship God. From the time of the tabernacle in the wilderness to the local church of today, God's people have worshiped Him. When David worshiped, he proclaimed, "Glory and honor are in his presence; strength and gladness are in his place" (1 Chron. 16:27). Honor and majesty go before God. They characterize His being, His glorious nature. Our God is a God of honor, majesty, strength, and gladness. "Make a joyful noise unto God, all ye lands: Sing forth the honor of his name: make his praise glorious" (Ps. 66:1-2).

When God is known in His works and ways, believers give praise to Him. When we worship God, we honor His work as Creator and Redeemer. We recognize His worthiness as Creator, Sustainer, and Redeemer. When we worship God, we adore Him in His perfect character. "Bless the Lord, O my soul. O Lord my God, thou art very great; thou art clothed with honor and majesty" (Ps. 104:1). The Lord is clothed with honor and majesty, which are His nature and character. The renowned hymnist Charles Wesley wrote:

Sovereign Father, heavenly King, Thee we now
presume to sing; Glad Thine attributes confess,
Glorious all, and numberless!"

Worship exalts the character of God. He is the one who has revealed Himself in such a wonderful way. Our worship centers on the honorable character of God. We adore Him for His faithfulness, goodness, justice, mercy, grace, and love. We stand in awe of His eternal nature, holiness, and power. We acknowledge His omnipresence and omniscience.

We honor God when we gather to worship. Both public and private worship provide an opportunity to praise God. Worship is expressing honor to God. It is declaring that He alone is worthy of praise. It is reverencing His name. Worship is an expression of a life surrendered to the Lord Jesus Christ.

Worship in Spirit and Truth

Jesus described the true nature of worship when he said to the woman at the well, "The hour cometh, and now is, when the true worshippers shall worship the Father in spirit and in truth: for the Father seeketh such to worship him. God is a Spirit: and they that worship him must worship him in spirit and in truth" (John 4: 23-24). When Jesus at that time described true worship, He helped us to understand its relationship to honor. *Worship is spiritual.* Genuine worship flows from the heart. "Bless the Lord, O my soul: and all that is within me" (Ps. 103:1). We may worship God imperfectly, but we must never be guilty of worshiping God insincerely.

Spiritual worship requires that we yield ourselves to the Holy Spirit of God. "No man can say that Jesus is the Lord, but by the Holy Ghost" (1 Cor. 12:3). The Spirit of God guides our worship. The Holy Spirit convicts, teaches, and encourages the believer in worship. As the Word of God is preached, the believer experiences the activity of the Holy Spirit personally. This is a little recognized aspect of worship. Worshiping God is a spiritual experience. It is a personal opportunity to encounter God and be transformed by the experience.

Our thoughts in worship are to be focused on spiritual things. "My heart is fixed, O God, my heart is fixed" (Ps. 57:7). Worship is establishing our thoughts and affections on spiritual things. Paul said that we are to set our minds on things above where Christ is seated. (See Col. 3:1-2). When we worship, our thoughts are to be focused on spiritual things. Whatever takes place in worship must assist the believer in achieving spiritual focus. The purpose of worship is not to entertain but to direct our thoughts toward God and to listen to what He says to us.

We present our bodies to God in worship. "Present your bodies a living sacrifice, holy, acceptable unto God, which is your reasonable service" (Rom. 12:1). True worshipers present their body to God for service. Worshipers in Old Testament times brought offerings to God to demonstrate their obedience and submission to Him. Doing that revealed their honor for the name of God. Believers in worship today must offer themselves. God wants our hearts, not our possessions. Worship is the act of presenting our bodies as living sacrifices to God.

The worshiper God seeks offers himself or herself as a living sacrifice to God to be used as He determines.

True worship is the experience of our spirit, with the Spirit of God agreeing that we are children of God. As we are drawn to God in worship, we express our thanks and dependence on Him. We worship His worthiness.

Jesus said also that worship is *truthful.* Those who worship God do so in truthfulness. Worship involves honesty about our real spiritual condition. Truthful worship is built on the truth of God's Word. The Word of God is central to worship. We receive the truth in worship through personal study of the Scriptures and the public preaching of the Word of God.

As we worship, we are to be spiritually clean or be made so in the experience. The psalmist wrote: "Who shall ascend into the hill of the Lord? or who shall stand in his holy place? He that hath clean hands, and a pure heart; who hath not lifted up his soul unto vanity, nor sworn deceitfully" (Ps. 24:3-4). The true worshiper is truthful before God in worship. Jesus reminded us that we can't worship God if there are relationship problems in our lives. "Therefore if thou bring thy gift to the altar, and there rememberest that thy brother hath aught against thee; Leave there thy gift before the altar, and go thy way; first be reconciled to thy brother, and then come and offer thy gift" (Matt. 5:23-24).

God seeks those who worship in spirit and truth as His worshipers. He receives our worship as an act of honor for Him. Worship is our expressing to God His absolute worthiness and our utter dependence on Him.

We honor God when we worship Him both privately and publicly. Throughout Scripture are examples of God's people worshiping the Lord in those ways. We should follow those examples. Honoring God is expressed in a life of spiritual, tasteful worship of God.

Worship in Heaven

Heaven will be a place of honoring God in unceasing worship. John the apostle gave us a glimpse of that glorious place: "And when those beasts give glory and honor and thanks to him that sat on the throne, who liveth for ever and ever, The four and twenty elders fall down before him that sat on the throne, and worship him that liveth for ever and ever, and cast their crowns before the throne, saying, Thou art worthy, O Lord, to receive glory and honor and power: for thou hast created all things, and for thy pleasure they are and were created" (Rev. 4:9-11).

Worship in heaven is focused on the throne of God.—This reminds us that we worship a God who reigns and rules supreme over all things. His dominion is absolute. He alone is worthy of worship. He is worthy because He is the creator of all things. He is worthy because everything exists by His will.

The picture of heavenly worship found in Scripture depicts the living creatures giving glory, honor, and thanks to Him who is seated on the throne. The One on the throne is seated, indicating that His reign is secure and certain over all things.

Three words express the honor to be given God in our worship. Glory expresses *reverence;* Honor—*recognition;* Thanks—*respect.* God alone deserves those expressions of honor in worship. Reverence can be translated "to bow down to the ground." This expressive language teaches the believer that worship is reverence for God. It is approaching God in recognition of His awesomeness, power, majesty, and might. Reverence in worship demonstrates submission to God and the believer's willingness to humble himself under the mighty hand of God. Reverence for God is an act of honoring God in worship.

Honor in worship seems to be confusing. Yet, when we consider that honor sometimes can be defined as recognition, there is a clear understanding about honor in worship. When we worship, we are recognizing that God deserves our time and attention. We are recognizing that we have needs that only He can meet. Believers in worship are honoring God by recognizing that only as they meet God do they offer acceptable sacrifice of life and possessions. Honor in worship is expressed when we stand to sing, bow our heads to pray, and stand for the reading of Scripture.

Thanks in worship expresses our respect for God. Thankfulness is essential worship. When we thank God, we respect Him for His blessings in our lives. Thankfulness demonstrates the believer's desire to appreciate the gifts of God. Worship without thankfulness is not honoring to God.

When the elders heard the heavenly song of praise, they responded in worship and "cast their crowns before the throne" (Rev. 4:10). That scriptural picture of worship in heaven reveals that as we come to worship God, we will lay everything before Him. It teaches us that worship must include glory, honor, praise, and thanksgiving for what God has done for us.

We learn from John's description of the worship of heaven the essential nature of worship. Worship is honoring God, who is worthy of all our worship. Worship is glorifying, honoring, and thanking God for His goodness and grace.

Jesus Christ will be worshiped and honored in heaven.—The myriad of heaven joined in praise to Jesus Christ, the Lamb of God. They declared that all power, riches, wisdom, strength, honor, glory, and blessing belong to Him. Jesus Christ is worthy of worship and honor. "And I beheld, and I heard the voice of many angels round about the throne and the beasts and the elders: and the number of them was ten thousand times ten thousand, and thousands of thousands; Saying with a loud voice, Worthy is the Lamb that was slain to receive power, and riches, and wisdom, and strength, and honor, and glory, and blessing. And every creature which is in heaven, and on the earth, and under the earth, and such as are in the sea, and all that are in them, heard I saying, Blessing and honor, and glory, and power, be unto him that sitteth upon the throne, and unto the Lamb for ever and ever" (Rev. 5:11-13).

Again the Bible says, "And all the angels stood round about the throne, and about the elders and the four beasts, and fell before the throne on their faces, and worshipped God, Saying, Amen: Blessing, and glory, and wisdom, and thanksgiving, and honor, and power, and might, be unto our God for ever and ever. Amen" (Rev. 7:11-12). The worship of heaven models worship for believers in this world. Heaven will be a place where God is honored in worship for eternity.

Jesus Christ is worshiped in heaven. As we worship the Lord Jesus Christ now and in the hereafter, we offer Him all power, riches, wisdom, strength, honor, glory, and blessing. He is worthy of all honor in worship. Even though this is hard to understand, the Bible says that ultimately all honor belongs to God.

Honor for God in the New Heaven and New Earth

The Bible says that when all things are made new, "The nations of them which are saved shall walk in the light of it: and the kings of the earth do bring their glory and honor into it. And the gates of it shall not be shut at all by day: for there shall be no night there. And they shall bring the glory and honor of the nations into it" (Rev. 21:24-26). The nations and the kings will bring their honor and glory into the New Jerusalem, demonstrating that all honor and glory belong to God. All earthly honor is only in stewardship from God. One day all the honor God has given to humanity will be given back to the only One who is worthy of honor and worship.

The Nature of Honor in Worship

The Bible reveals that worshiping God is honoring God. It is spiritual and truthful and the practice of believers in this world and of heaven. We honor God when we worship Him in reverence, adoration, and thanksgiving for His great character and works. Then, God honors those who worship Him.

We Honor God Through Stewardship

"Honor the Lord with thy substance, and with the firstfruits of all thine increase: So shall thy barns be filled with plenty, and thy presses shall burst out with new wine" (Prov. 3:9-10). This is the third great principle. Honoring God is expressed in our stewardship. The word stewardship is a management term. It describes the responsible management of another's possessions. God has given to everyone life and a measure of talents, gifts, family, and material possessions. *Stewardship is the act of faithfully managing the possessions God has given us.* Stewardship recognizes that everything is a gift from God and that God gives the increases in our lives. "For by me thy days shall be multiplied, and the years of thy life shall be increased" (Prov. 9:11).

God's Ownership

Honoring God through stewardship acknowledges that *all our possessions belong to God.* The Lord told Job, "Whatsoever is under the whole heaven is mine" (Job 41:11). The first principle of stewardship is understanding that *everything belongs to God.* He is the giver and sustainer of all things. Our life, family, material possessions, and personal abilities are gifts from God.

Our Responsibility

As we live in the recognition that God is the owner of all things, our *responsibility* is to be stewards of God's possessions. Jesus told a story to illustrate this principle of responsibility, saying, "Blessed are those servants, whom the lord when he cometh shall find watching: . . . And the Lord said, Who then is that faithful and wise steward, whom his lord shall make ruler over his household, to give them their portion of meat in due season?" (Luke 12:37,42).

Jesus reminded us that stewards are to remain faithful and responsible in their work. Many people live as if the possessions they have belong to them. Jesus reminded us that a steward is to be faithful and responsible even when his master is away on a journey. That is true for every believer. We honor God by our faithfulness in stewardship.

Our Accountability

Every steward will be accountable to the Lord Jesus Christ for his or her stewardship. Jesus ended the story of the faithful steward by saying: "Blessed is that servant, whom his lord when he cometh shall find so doing. Of a truth I say unto you, that he will make him ruler over all that he hath. But and if that servant say in his heart, My lord delayeth his coming; and shall begin to beat the menservants and maidens, and to eat and drink, and to be drunken; The lord of that servant will come in a day when he looketh not for him, and at an hour when he is not aware, and will cut him in sunder, and will appoint him his portion with the unbelievers. And that servant, which knew his lord's will, and prepared not himself, neither did according to his will, shall be beaten with many stripes. But he that knew not, and did commit things worthy of stripes, shall be beaten with few stripes. For unto whomsoever much is given, of him shall be much required: and to whom men have committed much, of him they will ask the more" (Luke 12: 43-48). Realize that you have been made accountable to God for many things. Remember that one day you will answer to God for your stewardship in regard to them.

It is important that believers take a personal account of the things that God has entrusted to them as stewards. God has entrusted us with our lives. We live today as a gift from God. He entrusts us to be good stewards of our life.

God had given us our time. Paul said that we are to be "Redeeming the time, because the days are evil" (Eph. 5:16). We must make sure that we are being good stewards of our time. Believers are good stewards as they invest in eternity by practicing good time management.

Every believer is given a measure of natural talent and spiritual gifts to be used to glorify God. The Bible says, "Glorify God in your body" (1 Cor. 6:20). God is glorified when we use our natural talents and spiritual gifts for the glory of God.

When we consider God and our finances, we often forget that God has given all believers a measure of financial responsibility. The issue is not how much we have but how faithful we are in our financial stewardship to God. Jesus observed the widow at the temple giving her little bit of money. He said, "Of a truth I say unto you, that this poor widow hath cast in more than they all: For all these have of their abundance cast in unto the offerings of God: but she of her penury hath cast in all the living that she had" (Luke 21:3-4).

We are accountable to give tithes and offerings from those finances that God has entrusted to us.

The relationships that we enjoy are a gift from God. As stewards, believers are to develop and grow the kinds of relationships that honor God. The relationships include our marriages, church relationships, and work relationships. The Christian steward strives to build strong, godly relationships with those whom God has placed in their lives.

For those who are faithful in stewardship, there is reward. God honors those who honor Him in their stewardship. But those who are disobedient and irresponsible face dishonor. The great principle of stewardship is found at the end of Jesus' story. "For unto whomsoever much is given, of him shall be much required: and to whom men have committed much, of him they will ask the more" (Luke 12:48). Our stewardship is faithfully managing what God has given us, knowing that someday we will answer to God for our stewardship. God's Word teaches us that all faithful stewards will be rewarded by the Lord.

Our Giving

We should honor God with our possessions. The act of tithing our material wealth is the biblical basis of honoring God in stewardship. It is the believer's responsibility as a steward to tithe one tenth of his income to God.

Honoring God by giving begins with the tithe. The first fruits of the crops and animals were to be given to God in Old Testament times. When we today honor God with the tithes and offerings of our possessions, we demonstrate our faith and obedience to God. When we give our money, we honor God for His goodness and care. Our giving is an expression of gratitude to God for the good gifts He has entrusted to us. Giving to God shows that we value His work with both our heart and our treasure.

The prophet Malachi reminded the people of Israel of how they had dishonored God by neglecting their tithes as an expression of their stewardship to God. The prophet declared, "Will a man rob God? Yet ye have robbed me. But ye say, Wherein have we robbed thee? In tithes and offerings. . . . Bring ye all the tithes into the storehouse, that there may be meat in mine house, and prove me now herewith, saith the Lord of hosts" (Mal. 3:8,10). The promise of blessing on those who honor God with the tithe is promised by the Lord: "I will . . . pour you out a blessing, that there shall not be room enough to receive it" (Mal. 3:10).

When Jesus pronounced His warning on the religious leaders of Israel, He declared that tithing is an essential part of honoring God but cannot be done to the neglect of showing mercy and justice. "Woe unto you, scribes and Pharisees, hypocrites! for ye pay tithe of mint and anise and cumin, and have omitted the weightier matters of the law, judgment, mercy, and faith: these ought ye to have done, and not to leave the other undone" (Matt. 23:23). Jesus said that tithing "ought ye to have done." Jesus never dismisses the believer from the responsibility of tithing.

In addition to tithes, we honor God with our offerings. Paul reminded the Corinthians of the importance of voluntary offerings in addition to the tithes. Offerings also express our stewardship to God. Paul was taking an offering for the suffering believers in Jerusalem when he wrote, "Moreover, brethren, we do you to wit of the grace of God bestowed on the churches of Macedonia; How that in a great trial of affliction the abundance of their joy and their deep poverty abounded unto the riches of their liberality. For to their power, I bear record, yea, and beyond their power they were willing of themselves; Praying us with much entreaty that we would receive the gift, and take upon us the fellowship of the ministering to the saints. And this they did, not as we hoped, but first gave their own selves to the Lord, and unto us by the will of God" (2 Cor. 8:1-5). Those words teach us that we honor God when we give our tithes and our offerings to the Lord.

A Christian investment banker compared his work and tithing in the following way. He said, "I invest people's money. I am a manager of their finances. I live off the 4-6 percent they pay me in commissions. I'm grateful for that and make a good living. God has been gracious and only asks of us 10 percent and leaves us with the 90 percent. God truly is gracious and good to us."

God's Honor for the Steward

When we honor God in stewardship, He honors us. Proverbs 3:10 describes God's blessing: "So shall thy barns be filled with plenty, and thy presses shall burst out with new wine." As we honor God with part of our substance, He provides for all of our needs. Moses reminded Israel that God would bless the obedience of His people: "The Lord shall command the blessing upon thee in thy storehouses, and in all that thou settest thine hand unto; and he shall bless thee in the land which the Lord thy God giveth thee" (Deut. 28:8).

That latter passage is not designed to promise riches. It testifies to the fact that God honors those who honor Him. The people of God always have found that to be true. King David testified to that truth when he wrote, "I have been young, and now am old; yet have I not seen the righteous forsaken, nor his seed begging bread" (Ps. 37:25).

When we honor God with our possessions, He provides what we need. As God's people give financially to their local church, they honor God. God wants us to give our tithes and offerings to the local church. The financial gifts are given in order that they be used for carrying out the ministries of the church and advancing the gospel around the world.

When we act as faithful stewards of the possessions God has entrusted to us, we honor God. Many people are dishonoring God in their stewardship. They live as if the things they have are their personal possessions, having forgotten that God is the owner of all things. Faithful management and accountability are the requirements of a God-honoring steward.

Evaluate how you are doing in this vital principle of honor. Are you giving God the best? Or, does He get the leftovers? To the measure we give, we honor God. God rewards those of us who give. God honors us as we give back to Him.

Application

When we honor God in discipleship, we express our submission to Jesus Christ as our Savior and Lord. When we honor God in worship, we express our reverence, adoration, and thanks to God for His wonderful character and His works on our behalf. When we honor God in stewardship, we express our dependence on God for all He has given us. Those are the three great principles of honoring God.

The eternal principle of honoring God must be our focus as believers. Honor begins with honor for God. When we honor God, He honors us. That principle is as true today as the day when the man of God spoke to Eli, the high priest. "For them that honor me I will honor, and they that despise me shall be lightly esteemed" (1 Sam. 2:30).

Study Guide

1. In your own words, summarize Eli's great sin. _____

2. Give examples of how believers today dishonor God by placing family and personal wants before God. _____
_____

3. Explain the biblical principle of honor. _____
_____

4. How does the honor the world gives compare to honor in the kingdom of God? _____
_____

5. Complete these statements:
   Honoring God begins with a commitment to _____
   Jesus deserves honor because He is _____
   In His discussion with the Pharisees, Jesus based His honor on His
   _____
   A life of discipleship _____
   _____.

6. The New Testament mentions four crowns, tokens of biblical honor, which remind us that when we stand before the Lord, it will be a time of honor and reward for believers. Identify the four crowns:
   A. The crown of the _____
   B. The crown of _____
   C. The crown of the _____
   D. The crown of the _____

7. Match the above crowns with the Scripture that recognizes the crown.
   _____ 1 Peter 5:1-4
   _____ Matthew 25: 21
   _____ James 1:12
   _____ 1 Corinthians 9:24-27

_____ Revelation 2:10
_____ 2 Timothy 4:8

8. We honor God through worship. Define worship. _____
_____

9. When we worship God we are honoring His perfect character. List some of the character qualities of God that we exalt in worship.
_____

10. How did Jesus describe the true nature of worship? _____
_____

11. Whose presence guides us in worship? _____

12. Explain what spiritual worship means to you. _____
_____

13. What significance does truth hold in our worship? _____
_____
_____

14. By honoring God through stewardship, we are acknowledging that—
_____
_____

15. Turn in the book to page 30, under the subtitle, "Our Accountability." Circle the five areas included in believers' personal accountability.

16. Beside each of these areas below name ways you are being a good steward:
    A. Life _____
    B. Time _____
    C. Talents/Gifts _____
    D. Finances _____
    E. Relationships_____

What Would You Do? It has come to your attention that several of the adult Sunday School teachers do not tithe. How would you explain to them the principle of honoring God through stewardship?

Chapter 3

Honoring Others

Be kindly affectioned one to another with brotherly love;
in honor preferring one another. Romans 12:10

Honoring God includes honoring others. The Bible describes honor for God being measured by our willingness to honor others, including those in positions of authority. This is a fundamental principle of honor. Honor requires an act of submission, which is humility before others. It requires humility to honor another. Jesus Christ lived his earthly life in humility. He modeled it for all believers. The ultimate act of Jesus' humility came in His emptying of Himself to be a man, but enthroned on the cross to die a humiliating death. (See Phil. 2:5-11.)

Jesus on one occasion observed that people were trying to get the best places to sit at a meal. "And he put forth a parable to those which were bidden, when he marked how they chose out the chief rooms; saying unto them, When thou art bidden of any man to a wedding, sit not down in the highest room; lest a more honorable man than thou be bidden of him; And he that bade thee and him come and say to thee, Give this man place; and thou begin with shame to take the lowest room. But when thou art bidden, go and sit down in the lowest room; that when he that bade thee cometh, he may say unto thee, Friend, go up higher: then shalt thou have worship in the presence of them that sit at meat with thee. For whosoever exalteth himself shall be abased; and he that humbleth himself shall be exalted" (Luke 14:7-11).

So, we learn that honoring others begins with humility. Humility of mind is the attitude necessary in honor. In fact, honor may be defined as *recognizing others as more significant than yourself.* That is a hard test. Biblical honor recognizes God and others as more significant than ourselves. That is a different message from what is heard in today's culture. People have gone their own way from the beginning. The Bible says, "All we like sheep have gone astray; we have turned every one to his own way" (Isa. 53:6). The world system demands self-centered, self-assertive actions, but the biblical model of honor is characterized by humility and submission. We are to treat others as more significant than ourselves. (See Phil. 2:3-4.) Until we obey that scriptural admonition, we are not practicing biblical honor.

Honor Those in Authority over You

Most people exhibit a great lack of understanding concerning authority. Perhaps that is why so little is known about honor. *Honoring God requires submitting to authority.* The history of the world is filled with examples of people who rejected authorities. Peter told us that the last days will be characterized by those who despise authorities. "The Lord knoweth how to deliver the godly out of temptations, and to reserve the unjust unto the day of judgment to be punished" (2 Pet. 2:9). Despising authority is a common characteristic in the world, church, and home today.

God has established judging authorities in the world so there will be order and protection. They are to be honored. In every realm, however, Jesus Christ is the one to be honored supremely because all judgment has been given to Him, according to John 5:22. He is the final authority in all things. His authority is universal over all creation.

It is critical that we learn to see the hand of God in the attitudes, actions, and directions of those God places over us. These God-ordained authorities include government authorities, pastoral authorities, and parental authorities. *They represent God's authority.*

When honor is shown to authorities, honor is given to God, also. Honoring authorities demonstrates our submission to God. It results in God's pleasure and blessing. As we learned in 1 Samuel 2:30, God honors those who honor Him.

To give such honor, we are to submit to God's created order in the world. The principle of submission carries over into many areas of our lives, but submission is difficult for many people. Yet, the Bible calls for honor to be shown to those in authority. Honor cannot be given without appropriate submission.

A lack of submission to authority is a clear sign of arrogance and is a sin against God. The Bible calls a lack of submission and obedience *rebellion.* When we, like King Saul, willfully resist the authorities whom

God has established, we are living in rebellion. Samuel reminded rebellious King Saul of that truth when he said, "For rebellion is as the sin of witchcraft, and stubbornness is as iniquity and idolatry" (1 Sam.15:23). Many of the spiritual problems present in believers' lives today can be attributed to a lack of submission to authority. Additionally, conflicts and troubles in relationships exist because of rebellion against God-ordained authorities. *Honoring God means submitting to His authorities.*

Position and Personality

Take a look at several issues related to submission to authority. First, recognize the difference between positions of authority and the people in those positions. God has established His authority in governments, the church, and the family. God designed those three broad institutions, but not every person in positions of authority in them is righteous and obedient to God.

Throughout the history of the church there have been persecution and martyrdom at the hands of government authorities. Authority has been abused in the church itself. In families, husbands and parents have misused the authority that God has given to them to use in the home. Nevertheless, the fact that authorities are God-ordained must be accepted and honored. The actions of the individuals in those positions don't lessen the importance of the positions. The positions of presidents, kings, governors, police, ministers, husbands, employers, and parents are positions of authority given by God, regardless of the persons who occupy them. How we respond to them is critical to the principle of honoring people in authority.

The apostle Peter illustrated the principle of submission to position, not to personality, when he wrote: "Servants, be subject to your masters with all fear; not only to the good and gentle, but also to the froward. For this is thankworthy, if a man for conscience toward God endure grief, suffering wrongfully. For what glory is it, if, when ye be buffeted for your faults, ye shall take it patiently? but if, when ye do well, and suffer for it, ye take it patiently, this is acceptable with God" (1 Pet. 2:18-20).

Peter said that the key to submission is having a "conscience toward God." When we submit to authorities, we are submitting as to the Lord. Even if we are wrongfully treated, we are "acceptable" before God when we submit to authorities. Our rightful submission to authorities over us results in honor to God

Jesus Christ's Submission to Authorities

Whatever the actions and attitudes of those in positions of authority may be, we must take responsibility for our reactions to them. Paul reminded us that the Lord Jesus Christ submitted to authorities and was crucified. He wrote, "Let this mind be in you, which was also in Christ Jesus: Who, being in the form of God, thought it not robbery to be equal with God: But made himself of no reputation, and took upon him the form of a servant, and was made in the likeness of men: And being found in fashion as a man, he humbled himself, and became obedient unto death, even the death of the cross" (Phil. 2:5-8).

Jesus Christ did not open his mouth before Pilate as He was wrongfully accused by the religious leaders. He submitted Himself even to the point of death. He recognized that God was controlling the situation for His own glory. Jesus left all believers an example of how we must willingly submit to the authorities in our lives. The early church understood that principle. Many gave their lives as evil authorities persecuted them. During this present century, many Christians have suffered at the hands of unjust authorities. They submitted themselves to authorities, recognizing that God ultimately will get the glory from whatever happens. Many have honored God and suffered in silent submission in order to honor God.

Submit, and Obey Authorities

The Lord Jesus *humbled* himself and became *obedient*. Those two words define the essence of honor to authorities in our lives. It is our responsibility to humble ourselves and obey them. Note that in many of the places in Scripture where honor is required, there is also a call to obedience.

In regard to *parental authority*, the Bible says: "Children, obey your parents in the Lord: for this is right. Honor thy father and mother; which is the first commandment with promise" (Eph. 6:1-2).

In regard to *pastoral authority*, the Bible says: "Obey them that have the rule over you, and submit yourselves: for they watch for your souls, as they that must give account, that they may do it with joy, and not with grief: for that is unprofitable for you" (Heb. 13:17). Paul's counsel to Timothy in 1 Timothy 5:17 points out that the elders who rule well and labor hard in word and teaching are to receive even double honor.

In regard to *government authority*, the Bible says: "Submit yourselves to every ordinance of man for the Lord's sake: whether it be to the king, as supreme; Or unto governors, as unto them that are sent by him for the punishment of evildoers, and for the praise of them that do well. For so is the will of God, that with well-doing ye may put to silence the ignorance of foolish men" (1 Pet. 2:13-15). Note the stress that Peter put on "well-doing."

God Controls Authorities

God uses authorities to carry out His work. God is at work in the world. He uses the authorities in governments, churches, and families to accomplish His purposes. Paul reminded us of that in Romans 13:4 when he said of government authorities: "For he is the minister of God to thee for good. But if thou do that which is evil, be afraid; for he beareth not the sword in vain: for he is the minister of God, a revenger to execute wrath upon him that doeth evil."

The Bible teaches that the Lord controls all authorities. "The king's heart is in the hand of the Lord, as the rivers of water: he turneth it whithersoever he will" (Prov. 21:1). Pharaoh released the children of Israel after God changed the mind of Pharaoh. Because God is working through authorities, we can be assured that God can change and redirect their decisions. *When we submit to authorities in our lives, we express faith that God will control the outcome of their decisions and that His will ultimately will be done.* As a result, God is honored by our submission and obedience to authorities.

Government Authorities

The Scriptures clearly reveal that God has established and controls government authorities. "Honor the king" (1 Pet. 2:17). "Let every soul be subject unto the higher powers. For there is no power but of God: the powers that be are ordained of God. Whosoever therefore resisteth the power, resisteth the ordinance of God: and they that resist shall receive to themselves damnation. . . . Wherefore ye must needs be subject, not only for wrath, but also for conscience sake. . . . Render therefore to all their dues: tribute to whom tribute is due; custom to whom custom; fear to whom fear; honor to whom honor" (Rom. 13:1-2,5,7).

As we submit to government authorities we honor God. Our submission recognizes God's ultimate authority over all things. Authorities exist and are sustained by God. When we resist authorities, we resist God. When we resist, judgment comes from the authorities. Showing respect and obedience to authorities in all other things is clearly a mark of honoring God. This is the clear meaning of Romans 13:2 when Paul said,

"Whosoever therefore resisteth the power, resisteth the ordinance of God." Therefore, it is essential that believers submit to the laws of the government. As Paul wrote, "Render therefore to all their dues: tribute to whom tribute is due; custom to whom custom; fear to whom fear; honor to whom honor" (Rom. 13:7).

The only exception to submitting to the government authorities comes when a believer is commanded to disobey God and not be free to share the gospel of Jesus Christ. When Peter and John were arrested not long after Pentecost, the rulers of Israel along with the religious authorities commanded them not to speak in the name of Jesus Christ. "And they called them, and commanded them not to speak at all nor teach in the name of Jesus. But Peter and John answered and said unto them, Whether it be right in the sight of God to hearken unto you more than unto God, judge ye. For we cannot but speak the things which we have seen and heard" (Acts 4:18-20). Again Peter and John were brought before the authorities who accused them: "Did not we straitly command you that ye should not teach in this name? and, behold, ye have filled Jerusalem with your doctrine, and intend to bring this man's blood upon us. Then Peter and the other apostles answered and said, We ought to obey God rather than men" (Acts 5:28-29).

Parental Authority

Honoring God is expressed as we honor our parents. The Bible presents God's requirement of honor for parents. "Honor thy father and thy mother, as the Lord thy God hath commanded thee; that thy days may be prolonged, and that it may go well with thee, in the land which the Lord thy God giveth thee" (Deut. 5:16). "Ye shall fear every man his mother, and his father, and keep my sabbaths: I am the Lord your God" (Lev. 19:3).

Jesus condemned the Pharisees for not honoring their parents. They invented a principle called "Corban," which means a gift to God, in order to keep from taking care of their parents. They did not honor their parents and therefore dishonored God. Jesus said to them, "Full well ye reject the commandment of God, that ye may keep your own tradition. For Moses said, Honor thy father and thy mother; and, Whoso curseth father or mother, let him die the death: But ye say, If a man shall say to his father or mother, It is Corban, that is to say, a gift, by whatsoever thou mightest be profited by me; he shall be free. And ye suffer him no more to do aught for his father or his mother; Making the word of God of none effect through your tradition, which ye have delivered: and many such like things do ye" (Mark 7:9-13).

Many people today do not honor their parents but instead, like those religious leaders, ignore their responsibility to honor their parents. All such actions dishonor God.

Honoring parents means showing reverence and respect for our parents. When we honor our parents, we honor God. Through our submission and obedience to them, we express honor for God and for them. God's commands remind us of His design for the home as a place for providing spiritual guidance.

The duty to honor father and mother and submit to them is also to be obeyed in blended families and by those who live in single-parent homes. We must remember that submission to parents does not include those situations when parents demand children to act in ways that are ungodly or harmful to them or to others. As we live our lives with our parents, we must seek to honor them as the parents whom God has given us.

Ministerial Authority

When we consider those who lead our congregations, we sometimes forget that they are God-called ministers. With God's leading, they are given the responsibility of overseeing the work of the church. The Book of Hebrews describes the biblical response to ministerial authority: "Obey them that have the rule over you, and submit yourselves: for they watch for your souls, as they that must give account, that they may do it with joy, and not with grief: for that is unprofitable for you" (Heb. 13:17).

Honoring ministerial authority means submitting to the ministers of the church and following their leadership. God has given ministers accountability concerning the people of God and their spiritual welfare. When we submit to the authority and leadership of the pastor and other ministers, we honor God. The position of minister is the position of God's authority established in the church. Such authority is not intended to be a dominating type of authority. It obviously can be misused. It is, however, God's design to give authority to ministers to guide the church in the work of ministry. This point is where dishonor for the position of minister begins for some people in the church. Such people argue that ministers are not the God-given authorities in the church. Scripture is clear that God expects both individual and group submission to ministerial authority. When we dishonor the ministers God called and gave to us, we dishonor God.

Honor One Another in Your Church

Paul reminded us that "Christ is the head of the church: and he is the saviour of the body" (Eph. 5:23). God carries out His work through the local church. The people of God utilizing their spiritual gifts minister to one another and carry out the Great Commission of our Lord. (See Matt 28:18-20.) The church should be a place of honor. The Bible tells us that we are to honor one another. "Be kindly affectioned one to another with brotherly love; in honor preferring one another" (Rom. 12:10). Believers honor one another when they show kind affection to each other. That happens when they conduct themselves with Christian love toward each other, remembering that the church is the family of God. Christians must show mutual respect and recognition for one another. In doing so, we honor God. Giving preference to one another is the biblical way to honor each other.

Ideas for honoring others in your church include:

1. Choose one person to honor each week. Honor that person privately by expressing your personal appreciation. You may include someone who has endured hardship, someone you know to be trustworthy, or someone who is a good parent.

2. Honor your Sunday School director, department director, teacher, or outreach leader with a private, personal word of affirmation or a small gift.

3. Honor the members of a church committee or a leadership team after they have worked especially hard and significantly on a project that may or may not have included you.

4. Give a word of appreciation to the people who share their talents in the worship services, including the organist, the pianist, the choir members, and the sound and light operators.

5. Write personal encouragement cards to someone in your church who has been a blessing to you. Do this each week.

"To put others along side of us, is generous and gracious, but to put them before us is divine. To halt that they might catch up, would be kindly, but to stop and step aside that others may pass before us in a race for honor and place, is far above nature. To prefer others before ourselves in heart and action, seems to bewilder and dizzy our untried heads. . . . This is the complete conquest of self, and requires a great victory."[1]

When we are in the presence of dignitaries, we give them preferential treatment. This should be the way we show honor to one another in our church.

Days of Honor in the Church

Here are some ideas for showing honor to others in your church. Many churches practice honoring one another by giving special recognition to various groups in the church throughout the year. The following list is an example of how a church can establish days of honor. These recognition days can be developed as part of the Sunday evening services throughout the year. Special gifts and presentations can be made to honor the members of the church who serve in these areas of responsibility. Such groups to be honored may include:

— Young Adult Sunday School teachers
— Preschool ministry leaders
— TeamKID leaders
— Children's Sunday School teachers
— Youth Sunday School teachers
— Women's Ministry leaders
— Student Ministry leaders
— Median Adult Sunday School teachers
— Choir and orchestra members and directors
— Senior Adult Sunday school teachers
— Single Adult Sunday School leaders
— Men's Ministry leaders
— Ministerial staff and their families
— Student music ministry leaders
— Ushers, greeters, and information booth workers
— Bus ministry workers
— Kitchen crew
— Deacons
— Building and grounds workers

Honor the Widows

Honoring one another in the church specifically includes giving honor to widows. Paul wrote: "Honor widows that are widows indeed. But if any widow have children or nephews, let them learn first to shew piety at home, and to requite their parents: for that is good and acceptable before God" (1 Tim. 5:3-4).

Widows are to be recognized and cared for by the church. This expresses honor to God. *When we honor widows, we honor God.* In the early church, honor for widows included taking care of them financially. Honor for these special women includes respect and financial support.

We obviously should remember also the men who have lost wives. In addition, there may be others in financial need among the church membership. We show honor when we take care of people in their weakness.

Examine your church, and evaluate the extent to which you honor one another. When we honor one another in the church, we honor God.

Honor in the Workplace

We must honor God in our workplace. It may come as a surprise to you that God desires us to honor Him in our jobs, but it is true. We must evaluate our honor for God at our jobs. We spend large amounts of time in the workplace. The Bible tells us that God is interested in our work. The relationships we have with those in authority over us at our work are important to God.

We honor God when we honor our supervisors and executives.—Paul wrote, "Let as many servants as are under the yoke count their own masters worthy of all honor, that the name of God and his doctrine be not blasphemed" (1 Tim. 6:1). Servants were treated as property by their masters during the first century. They were, however, to show "all honor" to their masters in order that the name of God not be blasphemed. We are to honor those who are placed over us in the workplace.

In showing honor to our employers, Paul indicated what is required. He wrote to Titus, "Exhort servants to be obedient unto their own masters, and to please them well in all things; not answering again; Not purloining, but shewing all good fidelity; that they may adorn the doctrine of God our Saviour in all things" (Titus 2:9-10).

As we honor our employers, we must show honor to them by our *obedience.* In obeying, we honor God. We are not to respond in anger to employer requests. We are to abstain from stealing from our employers. When we so honor our employers, we show ourselves honest and witness to the glory of God.

Paul wrote also to the church at Ephesus about the responsibility to honor our employers: "Servants, be obedient to them that are your masters according to the flesh, with fear and trembling, in singleness of your heart, as unto Christ; Not with eye-service, as men-pleasers; but as the servants of Christ, doing the will of God from the heart; With good will doing service, as to the Lord, and not to men: Knowing that whatsoever good thing any man doeth, the same shall he receive of the Lord, whether he be bond or free" (Eph. 6:5-8).

Paul's words explain that our honor at work is not done solely for the employer or owner, but for the Lord. We do honor them with sincerity of heart, recognizing that it is God's will that we be obedient to our employers. Paul revealed the principle of honor that will follow: "Whatsoever good thing any man doeth, the same shall he receive of the Lord" (Eph. 6:8). Whatever we do in honor to those for whom we work, the Lord will return to us. God honors those who honor their employers. While our honor is to God and not to people, God expects us to show honor to those he has placed over us.

The employer or business owner is to honor employees.—Those who are supervisors over others should remember that honor is to be given to the employee. When we honor our employees, God honors us. Paul wrote, "And, ye masters, do the same things unto them, forbearing threatening: knowing that your Master also is in heaven; neither is there respect of persons with him"(Eph. 6:9).

The employer must give honor to employees as to Christ. Honor for the employees must be sincere and from the heart. The employer is accountable to the Master, the Lord Jesus Christ. When employers honor their employees, God honors them. They receive back from the Lord what they have given in honor.

As we honor one another in the workplace, we honor God. The most difficult place for many to be a Christian witness is in the workplace. Even so, God's will is that honor be shown in this situation.

Honor Your Mate in Your Marriage

God has created the family for His glory. The family provides future generations of godly children who will worship and serve the Lord. Thus, the family is God's basic building block for His world. God told Adam, "Be fruitful, and multiply, and replenish the earth, and subdue it: and have dominion over the fish of the sea, and over the fowl of the air, and over every living thing that moveth upon the earth" (Gen. 1:28). God is honored when families are spiritually strong and relationships within them are right.

At the heart of the family is the relationship between the husband and wife. God intended that marriage consist of one man and one woman for life. Scripture records, "Therefore shall a man leave his father and his mother, and shall cleave unto his wife: and they shall be one flesh" (Gen. 2:24). Perhaps nothing better demonstrates the dynamics of honor for one another than the marriage relationship. The Bible describes the relationship as one of both submission and leadership: "Wives, submit yourselves unto your own husbands, as unto the Lord. For the husband is the head of the wife, even as Christ is the head of the church: and he is the saviour of the body. Therefore as the church is subject unto Christ, so let the wives be to their own husbands in every thing. Husbands, love your wives, even as Christ also loved the church, and gave himself for it; . . . Nevertheless let every one of you in particular so love his wife even as himself; and the wife see that she reverence her husband" (Eph. 5: 22-25, 33).

This passage shows that honor must exist in a marriage relationship. Marriages that honor God are characterized by submission and leadership like that of the church submitting to Christ. Submission honors God.

It recognizes and affirms God's design for marriage. Peter wrote concerning this matter of honor in marriage: "Likewise, ye husbands, dwell with them according to knowledge, giving honor unto the wife, as unto the weaker vessel, and as being heirs together of the grace of life; that your prayers be not hindered" (1 Pet. 3:7). When wives submit to the leadership of their husbands, they honor God. When men honor their wives, placing them above all others, they honor God. The Bible is clear that God will not honor a man if he does not honor his wife. Peter said that a man's prayers would be hindered if he did not honor his wife.

Marriages characterized by both submission and respect are honorable before God. Such relationships honor God, who planned and purposed the family to glorify Him.

Principles of Honoring Others

God fulfills His purposes in the world through authorities, churches, and families. He is at work through those agencies. God will not be honored unless there is a willing submission to honor others in the special relationships we have with them. Perhaps that is the reason many churches and marriages fail and have lost the favor and blessing of God. The Lord made it clear to Eli, "For them that honor me I will honor" (1 Sam. 2:30). It is time to take a careful look at the degree of honor we give one another. How can we honor God if we cannot honor one another?

When God wants to demonstrate honor, He does it through the relationships of His people. Honoring others honors God. We develop an attitude of humility when we are able to recognize the need to see others as superior to ourselves. The God-given authorities in our lives remind us of the opportunities we have to submit to God's direction and authority. Churches honor God as members show preference for one another in love. Families honor God when husbands and wives demonstrate honor for one another. Doing so not only teaches their children this vital principle, it glorifies God.

Application

Honor for God is lived out in our daily relationships. Take an account of your relationships. How are you doing in regard to honoring others?
- Are you living in submission and obedience to those who are over you?
- How do you show preference for others in church?
- How does your church honor widows and others in their weakness?

• How do you honor your mate in your marriage?

As we honor others whom God has placed in our lives, we honor God. "For them that honor me I will honor, and they that despise me shall be lightly esteemed" (1 Sam. 2:30).

[Edward M. Bounds, *Heaven* (New York: Fleming H. Revell Company, 1921), 96.

Study Guide

1. In Luke 14:7-11, what lesson is Jesus teaching about honoring others?
_____

2. Honoring others begins with humility. In your own words define humility. _____
_____

Give an example of the actions of a humble person. _____
_____

3. Explain why submission to those in authority over us bears a direct relationship to our honor of God's authority. _____
_____

4. In 1 Peter 2:18-20 what does Peter teach about actions that are "acceptable" with God? _____
_____

5. Identify times in Jesus' life where He submitted to those in positions of authority. _____
_____

6. Dr. Miller states that submission and obedience define the essence of giving honor to the authorities in our lives. In your own words, explain that statement. _____
_____
_____

7. Read Romans 13:4 and Proverbs 21: 1. What do we know about the authorities in our world? _____
_____

8. Personalize Hebrews 13:17 for you and your church._____

_____

9. How does the way we honor our ministers and others in our church affect our relationship with the Lord? _____

_____

10. Turn to page 44, chapter 3, under "Honor One Another in Your Church." Circle two ways that you choose to honor others in your church

11. Evaluate your "honor" lifestyle in the areas listed below. Use the scale: 0- 5, with 0 being complete dishonor and 5 perfect honor (only Jesus rates a 5!).

Government authorities	_____
Parents	_____
Ministers	_____
Church members	_____
Lay workers at church	_____
Widows	_____
Supervisors at work	_____
Coworkers	_____
Marriage partner	_____

As you evaluate your practice of honoring others, look at the list above and put a star beside people in your life whom you need to honor.

What Would You Do? You are a member of the Church Council. As you are planning the calendar for the coming year, you do not see any time set aside for honoring lay workers in the church. What would be your recommendations?

Chapter 4

Honoring God's Ministers

Let the elders that rule well be counted worthy
of double honor. 1 Timothy 5:17

Current Conditions Among Ministers

The situation facing many pastors and other ministers is alarming. There is among our churches a growing lack of honor for these God-called leaders. Churches of all sizes have been blessed with one or more faithful, dependable ministers to lead them. The ministers are content to work for the Lord wherever He sends them, despite adversity and sacrifice. They are true soldiers of the Lord. Regrettably, ministers are not being honored in many churches today.

Whenever you ask ministers about their needs, they are somewhat hesitant to respond. They feel uncomfortable in talking about their needs and hurts. Furthermore, some church members seem to be oblivious to the challenges and difficult circumstances faced by ministers and their families every day. That does not change the fact that the needs of ministers are real and the pressures extreme. Honor for ministers has never been needed like it is today.

Over the past 20 years there have been serious discussions about the difficult conditions ministers face in their work. The following statistics from two surveys, one by the Fuller Institute and the other by *Leadership* magazine, portray a picture of ministry conditions that ministers face on a daily basis:
• 90 percent of ministers work more than 46 hours per week.
• 90 percent of ministers feel inadequately trained to cope with

51

the ministry demands they face.

• 70 percent have lower self-esteem about themselves in ministry than when they started in the ministry.

• 40 percent report serious conflicts with a church member at least once a month.

• 70 percent do not have someone they consider a close friend (Fuller Institute).

• 94 percent of ministers feel pressured to have ideal families (*Leadership*, Fall 1992).

For some ministers today there is a debate in their minds about whether the ministry is worth the cost. They feel unappreciated, undervalued. One minister told a friend, "I'm quitting; I can't take the abuse any longer."

How do we respond to such situations in our churches? Are you aware of such feelings on the part of your ministers? You may never have considered that they are struggling. The fact remains that the statistics cited reflect the feelings of many ministers.

A leading counselor who works with discouraged ministers said that many ministers struggle with low self-esteem related to their ministry work. "We are in a high-demand, low-stroke profession in a culture that does not value our product or our work. We labor among people with unrealistic expectations, and deep inside we expect far more from ourselves and the church."[1]

The LifeWay Church Leadership Division of LifeWay Christian Resources conducted a survey among pastors in the Southern Baptist Convention. The results describe the conditions among ministers.

• 50 percent of the pastors' wives work outside the home

• 45 percent of the pastors have served in their current church for fewer than five years

• 10 percent have served in their current church for more than 15 years

• 75 percent earn less than $50,000 per year in salary

• 70 percent receive retirement and health insurance

• 17 percent receive annual recognition from the church to honor them on their annual church anniversary.

How can a church assist its ministers and reduce their pressures? Many of the issues can be solved when the church honors the ministers whom God has given them. Some people will read this information and make excuses. Others will be moved by the information but will feel powerless to change the situation. Some will be challenged to consider what their church is doing in becoming more sensitive to the needs of the ministers.

In most instances, the faithfulness of ministers is not questionable in spite of the working conditions they face. Regrettably, some ministers have damaged the credibility of church leaders. Even so, there remains an army of committed pastors and other ministers who listen to God and lead their churches to follow Him. They should be honored.

In a recent conference of Christians, all the ministers were invited to the front of the room to be recognized and honored. As the ministers made their way forward, the assembled others rose to their feet, clapping and cheering for them. How beautiful!

A prominent pastor told of a time when he returned from vacation and the church presented him with a plaque signed by over six hundred church members. Each person pledged to pray for him every day during the next year. How encouraging!

Those are only two examples of how churches and other Christian groups have honored ministers. How does your church honor your ministers? Honoring them is crucial for good relationships within the church.

God-called Ministers

Perhaps the best place to begin a discussion of the church's responsibility for honoring ministers is by understanding that God *calls* ministers to their work. The Scriptures are full of examples of God's call of leaders to guide the work of His people. In the Old Testament, figures like Moses, Joshua, Samuel, David, the prophets, Nehemiah, and Daniel were called by God to lead the children of Israel.

God always calls out leaders for His people. Isaiah heard and responded to God's call. "I heard the voice of the Lord, saying, Whom shall I send, and who will go for us? Then said I, Here am I; send me" (Isa. 6:8). Whether Moses looking at the burning bush, Samuel as a boy hearing God calling in the night, or Nehemiah sensing an urgency to go back and rebuild Jerusalem, God calls out ministers to guide His people.

Examples in the New Testament tell the same story. Jesus called disciples to follow Him. He spent three years instructing those disciples that they might lead the early church. Christ called Paul to service. Paul wrote, "But when it pleased God, who separated me from my mother's womb, and called me by his grace, To reveal his Son in me, that I might preach him among the heathen" (Gal. 1:15-16). God continues to call out leaders today.

God-called ministers are essential for the church. God equips those He calls for the work of ministry. Church members should be aware that ministers have been specially called by God and equipped under His guidance to lead the church. They should be recognized as God-called ministers and treated with respect.

At the end of every sermon, most preachers issue an invitation to respond to Christ. Yet another invitation ought to be explicitly extended at the same time—an invitation to respond to God's call to Christian leadership. Every church has had a number of people who through the years have responded to God's call to be a minister, including some to be a missionary. It is a sign of God's blessing for a church to see God call ministers to His work.

What does your church do to honor those who have been called to Christian service? Most churches have never paused to consider the blessing of God in calling out leaders.

In churches all across the country men and women sense that God is calling them into some aspect of ministry. The people are from all backgrounds and ages. Some have surrendered to God after serving in other careers, while still others are giving their early years to God in service.

We don't always realize the importance of this calling until it impacts us personally. A deacon said, "I never thought much about the ministry until God called my son to be a minister." Perhaps you haven't thought much about this important issue. God-called leaders deserve special honor from the people in their church.

God's Gifts to the Church

Nothing encourages the heart more than to think about the gifts God has given to the church. How grateful we are for God's gift of righteousness. "Therefore as by the offence of one judgment came upon all men to condemnation; even so by the righteousness of one the free gift came upon all men unto justification of life" (Rom. 5:18).

The *gift of eternal life* is ours through our belief in what Jesus Christ accomplished on the cross, according to John 11:25. In addition, Paul wrote, "The wages of sin is death; but the gift of God is eternal life through Jesus Christ our Lord" (Rom. 6:23).

We live in grace and without condemnation. God's grace sometimes is described as God's riches at Christ's expense. Grace is what God has shown to us instead of wrath. His grace forgives, restores, renews, and encourages the believer. Oh, the joy of the *gift of grace!* What a wonderful privilege we believers have in free access to God through Jesus Christ the Lord. "For by grace are ye saved through faith; and that not of yourselves: it is the gift of God" (Eph. 2:8).

The church operates as a result of *spiritual gifts* that have been given to every believer by the Holy Spirit. "For as we have many members in one body, and all members have not the same office: So we, being many, are one body in Christ, and every one members one of another. Having then gifts differing according to the grace that is given to us, whether prophecy, let us prophesy according to the proportion of faith" (Rom. 12:4-6). The church has been blessed by God with wonderful gifts. We have everything we need freely given by our Lord Jesus Christ.

God has provided yet another gift that we tend not to consider. God has provided the church with the *gift of leadership.* "And he gave some, apostles; and some, prophets; and some, evangelists; and some, pastors and teachers; For the perfecting of the saints, for the work of the ministry, for the edifying of the body of Christ" (Eph. 4:11-12).

When Christ ascended, He gave the church spiritual gifts from the Holy Spirit to equip them for the work of the ministry. He gave the church the gift of leadership to direct the ministry. God has given ministers to your church as a gift from Him. When we honor our ministers, we are thanking God for His gift of leadership to the church.

Double Honor for Church Ministers

The auditorium of the average church is fairly standard in its appearance. Those who have gone to church for any length of time have grown accustomed to the appearance and surroundings of the building. Inside the auditorium is a reminder of the importance of giving honor to the God-called ministers of the church.

Two or more chairs sit on a raised platform at the front of most church auditoriums. The chairs are seats of honor. When people of the congregation come into the auditorium, they do not sit in those chairs. They are for the ministers of the church. They symbolize the biblical principle of honor for ministers. The chairs are tangible reminders of the honor that the church should give to its worthy leaders.

In giving young Timothy instructions for church order, Paul reminded him of the importance of teaching the church to honor its ministers. Paul commanded, "Let the elders that rule well be counted worthy of double honor, especially they who labour in the word and doctrine. For the scripture saith, Thou shalt not muzzle the ox that treadeth out the corn. And, The labourer is worthy of his reward. Against an elder receive not an accusation, but before two or three witnesses" (1 Tim. 5:17-19).

Understanding what Paul meant in that passage is important. Though the Bible mentions several groups to whom honor is to be shown, only one group is to receive double honor. The Bible says that the worthy ministers of the church are to be the recipients of double honor!

The Identity of the Elder

When Paul used the term "elder," who did he mean? There is much confusion today concerning the terms used to describe ministers in the church. The terms *elder* and *bishop* are interchangeable words in the New Testament. They describe functional differences in the work of the leader of the church, not differences in office. The Bible does not teach a hierarchy of ministry positions. When Paul talked about the offices of the church, he identified only two. The office of bishop, or elder, and the office of deacon. (See 1 Tim. 3:1-13). When Paul spoke of elders, he referred to bishops. The bishops were given the responsibility to oversee the entire work of the church. The Book of Hebrews states, "Obey them that have the rule over you, and submit yourselves: for they watch for your souls, as they that must give account, that they may do it with joy, and not with grief: for that is unprofitable for you" (Heb. 13:17). The writer of Hebrews explained that a bishop watches over the church and must give an account to God for his leadership of the church.

The church at Philippi had multiple bishops, or ministers. Paul wrote, "To all the saints in Christ Jesus which are at Philippi, with the bishops and deacons" (Phil. 1:1). The elders at Ephesus were called bishops. Paul said to them, "Take heed therefore unto yourselves, and to all the flock, over the which the Holy Ghost hath made you overseers, to feed the church of God, which he hath purchased with his own blood" (Acts 20:28). When Paul wrote to Titus instructing him to appoint *(kathistemi)* elders, he then described the qualifications for a bishop: "For this cause left I thee in Crete, that thou shouldest set in order the things that are wanting, and ordain elders in every city, as I had appointed thee: . . . For a bishop must be blameless, as the steward of God; not selfwilled, not soon angry, not given to wine, no striker, not given to filthy lucre" (Titus 1:5,7).

Peter addressed the elders and described their responsibilities: "Feed the flock of God which is among you, taking the oversight thereof, not by constraint, but willingly; not for filthy lucre, but of a ready mind" (1 Pet. 5:2). When we use the term *minister* or *pastor,* we are referring to those described in the New Testament as bishops or elders.

Elders as Rulers

What does Paul mean by the phrase "rule well" in 1 Timothy 5:17? The role of the first-century elder as a leader is crucial in understanding how to honor the ministers of the church today. The word *rule* in the passage means "to be at the head." It describes the general superintendence of pastors. It is used in other Greek literature to describe the art and act of giving general management direction to persons in organizations. The word *rule* is not meant to imply dictatorial domination. Paul identified the minister's function as that of leader and teacher of the church. Peter said when writing to the leaders concerning their qualifications for their office, "Neither as being lords over God's heritage, but being ensamples to the flock" (1 Pet. 5:3). To "rule well" means to guide effectively the entire work of the church. Paul reminded Timothy that the church is to show double honor to the ministers who "rule well." Ministers who rule well are those who are doing the God-assigned tasks of leading and teaching the church.

Even so, the word *ruler* describes the one who is the head, thus implying a *position of authority*. Ministers are the rulers of the church. For many in today's churches, that statement sounds strange and un-Baptistic. Yet, it expresses the truth of Scripture. God has placed the minister as the authority over the church under the lordship of Jesus Christ. *When we honor such leaders of the church, we honor God.*

The Meaning of Double Honor

The meaning of the words *double honor* in 1 Timothy 5:17 establishes a foundation for the practice of honoring ministers in the local church.

The word *double* is used in various places in the Bible. In Deuteronomy 21:17, the firstborn was to receive a double portion of the inheritance: "But he shall acknowledge the son of the hated for the firstborn, by giving him a double portion of all that he hath: for he is the beginning of his strength; the right of the firstborn is his." Elisha asked Elijah for a double portion of his spirit. "And it came to pass, when they were gone over, that Elijah said unto Elisha, Ask what I shall do for thee, before I be taken away from thee. And Elisha said, I pray thee, let a double portion of thy spirit be upon me" (2 Kings 2:9). In Hebrews 3:3, Jesus Christ is described as receiving "more" honor than Moses. "For this man was counted worthy of more glory than Moses, inasmuch as he who hath builded the house hath more honor than the house."

Double in biblical context means more or greater than what is given to others. Therefore, while we honor authorities, one another, employers, widows, and mates, we should give greater honor to the God-called ministers of the church who rule well. *Double honor is for the ministers God gives the church.*

The term *honor* may be translated as "remuneration." "It probably consisted of the twin benefits of honor or respect and financial remuneration. The fact that pay was at least included shows that those who gave leadership to spiritual affairs could expect financial support from the church (cf 2 Cor. 11:8-9, Gal. 6:6)."[2]

God intends that the ministers of His church be honorably rewarded for their labors. Paul continued in 1 Timothy 5:17 to highlight "they who labour in the word and doctrine." The work that ministers have been given by God is labor. They are to guide the direction of the church and labor to teach and preserve the church in the truth of God's Word. The minister does that work through his important teaching and preaching ministries.

There are those in the church today who do not appreciate the labor of ministers. In considering how they are going to pay their leaders, every church should remember Paul's admonition. This was his intention: *Ministers deserve both double honor and remuneration on a scale commensurate with the honor given them.* What a difference it would make in a church if the people sought to make their ministers among the best paid people in the church.

Once in a church personnel committee meeting the pastor's salary was being discussed. A recommendation was made that his salary be increased because it was below the median salary of the church members. One committee member was opposed to a salary increase. His reason was simple to him—a low salary kept the pastor humble. The dissenter thought that it was the responsibility of the personnel committee to keep the pastor poor and humble.

Such an attitude is prevalent in some churches today. It represents the tragedy of dishonoring the ministers God has given the church. "Double honor" is showing great respect to the ministers and financially supporting them on the basis of the spiritual work they are doing.

How does your church measure up in showing double honor to your ministers? When you consider their salary and benefits, are they paid adequately for their labors? When a church honors the ministers God gives them, the people honor God. The principle of 1 Samuel 2:30 is true: "Them that honor me I will honor."

Suggestions for Double Honor

Perhaps no picture better illustrates the act of honor than the awarding of the medals at the Olympic Games. The triumphant athletes stand on raised platforms and are honored with flowers, medals, and applause from the crowd. This scene depicts the actions of honor: *respect, recognition,* and *rewards.* Like in the Olympic Games, churches need to show honor to those who deserve it. This section provides some illustrations of ways in which your church can demonstrate double honor for your ministers.

Respect, recognition, and rewards are an easy way to remember the essentials of honor when focusing on honoring ministers. Each of those words represents one of the aspects of biblical honor. They capture the essence of what God intends for the church to do in regard to showing honor to each leader. Double honor for ministers includes the giving of respect, recognition, and rewards.

Respect

A pastor of a small church was embarrassed because of his wife's health. She had been hospitalized with some serious emotional problems. The church lay leaders determined that it was not appropriate for their church to have a pastor with such a situation in his home. They determined to force the pastor to resign. He refused because he believed that God was not finished with him at the church. His situation was also strained with two children who obviously had needs. He was faithfully caring for his wife, the children, and the work of the church.

When the pastor refused to resign, some of the powerful lay leaders took things into their own hands. Ignoring the negative impact their action would have on the pastor's family, especially the children, they arbitrarily moved the family's belongings out of the church parsonage and notified the man that he no longer was the pastor of the church. The dismissal and eviction occurred during the Christmas season. When a few compassionate others heard about the situation, several offerings were taken to help the man and his family until he could relocate in another church ministry.

This story illustrates the reality that faces some ministers. They serve but receive little respect. One long-time pastor made this observation about the current level of respect for ministers and their ministry:

I have a friend I have known and loved for thirty years. During that period of time we have been inseparable. Our friendship has deepened as my appreciation for this friend has intensified.

In recent years my friend has come upon hard times. We have continued to get along beautifully, but others have begun to misunderstand and malign. It has hurt me to hear all the ugly things being said. Even though my friend has done nothing wrong and has taken the brunt of unfair, exaggerated, and sarcastic remarks—not to mention all the unfounded and caustic accusations—there seems to be no letup. It has gotten so bad on occasions I've wondered if there can be a full recovery. In spite of all that has been said against my dear friend, our commitment has remained firm and true for thirty-five years.

My friend is the ministry.[3]

George Gallup said: "Most institutions and leaders in America have been taking a hit in recent years from the public who have been losing confidence in them. There was a time when members of the clergy were usually the most respected members of their community. . . . Currently, a slim majority of the public rates the honesty and ethical standards of the clergy as 'very high' or 'high', but one person in three considers them only average, and one in ten thinks they are 'low' or 'very low.'"[4]

You may think that everyone would believe that respect for ministers exists among Christians. Regrettably, that is not true. Paul said to the Ephesian church, "Be ye kind one to another, tenderhearted, forgiving one another, even as God for Christ's sake hath forgiven you" (Eph. 4:32). Ministers need to experience the kindness and tenderness that comes from a loving church. There are several areas in which we should respect the minister.

When we respect the office to which the minister has been called, we honor God.—Paul wrote to Timothy, "This is a true saying, If a man desire the office of a bishop, he desireth a good work" (1 Tim. 3:1). The "position" of minister is an honorable one in the church. Those who fill the position give general oversight to the work of the church and preach and teach the Word of God that the church might grow in Christlikeness. Even though there are differences in personality types among those who fill the position of minister, all should be honored because God has called them to the work.

Each minister given your church was called by God. The church affirms the call of God on the life of those who serve as a minister of the church. A vote is taken by the congregation in most of our churches when a minister is selected. Church members believe that those who serve as ministers are called of God. We affirm that they have given evidence of a call from God to leadership and are qualified to serve in a ministry position. How can it be that a church can vote to affirm God's call for a minister to serve and then dishonor that person?

When we respect the humanity of ministers, we honor God.—Why do we expect perfection of our ministers while accepting our own limitations and failures? The expectations for ministers in many situations are unrealistic. An old deacon said to a young pastor, "If I haven't disappointed you yet, just wait. I will real soon." Perhaps we need a new bumper sticker for our cars that reads 'Pastors aren't perfect; they are forgiven!' In honoring our ministers, we must be aware of their humanity.

The biblical qualifications for bishops speak of high personal standards, but nothing is said about their being perfect. The development of character is a lifelong process for both the believer and the ministerial leader. When Paul addressed the church at Philippi, he wrote, "Being confident of this very thing, that he which hath begun a good work in you will perform it until the day of Jesus Christ" (Phil. 1:6). Paul in this message assured believers that God finishes what He begins in them. That is true in ministers' lives as well. No minister is perfect. Everyone has areas that need improvement. God continues to work in their lives.

You may hear church members say that a certain pastor or staff member has disappointed them or hurt them. Sometimes when people say these things they are using the minister's disappointing actions as an excuse for their own lack of faithfulness and service to God. The fact remains that relationships at times can be difficult between ministers and members. Paul's words in Philippians 1:6 remind us that God hasn't finished with any of us yet.

Years ago in a conference for youth, the teenagers were given buttons with some letters printed on them. The letters presented a good way of thinking about how we should respect our ministers and accept their humanity. The saying was "Please be patient. God is not finished with me yet." We must be patient with our ministers. God is still working on them.

When we honor our ministers, we respect their humanity and allow them the opportunity for God to work in their lives. "Forgiving one another, even as God for Christ's sake hath forgiven you" (Eph. 4:32). Even in cases of serious offensive actions and sins, we need to forgive and accept the ministers God gives our church, recognizing that God can forgive them and continue working to make them more like Christ.

When we respect the families of ministers, we honor God.—The Bible
has only a limited amount to say about the families of the ministers in
the church. In 1 Timothy 3:2,4 a statement of the qualifications for the
office of bishop, or pastor, includes that he be "the husband of one wife"
and "One that ruleth well his own house, having his children in subjection with all gravity."

The few scriptural references to the families of ministers remind us
that God has high standards for them. The minister sets an example in his
home for how God intends for Christian families to live. When church
members do not respect a minister's family, they dishonor God, also.

The minister's wife should be respected and honored. These women
serve by the side of their husbands in all kinds of situations. They are for
the most part overlooked and underappreciated, sometimes even by the
minister and many people in the church. Some frightening information
about the struggles of ministers' wives recently has been documented.

A random survey of ministers' wives by Focus on the Family
revealed that more than half of those surveyed were severely depressed.
H.B. London in an interview with James Dobson said: "These wives have
reasons to be depressed in many situations. They are expected not to
express themselves about anything. They are supposed to sit in the corner
while their husbands run the show. And they die by inches when they see
their husbands come home, and sit in a chair, and stare into space. They
ask, 'is it worth it all? Are we doing any good? Does anyone care? Will it
ever change?' And most of the obvious answers are even more frightening
than the questions."[5]

Ministers' wives tend to suffer from loneliness. A survey of 226 pastors' wives by Duane Alleman in a publication out of Fuller Seminary report-
edly revealed that 45 percent of them have no close friends within their
churches. Almost half of them feel constrained in developing close friends in
the church. The fault cannot be deduced. It surely is compound and multi-
farious. The effectiveness of some ministers has been called into question
based on studies of the minister's family and the way the family members
conduct themselves. This is a pressure point for any minister's family.

A pastor of a small church in a county seat town lived in the church
parsonage. He and his family enjoyed the home and appreciated the
church for providing it. Once they were out of town for the day on a family activity. When they returned, they discovered that their house was being
used for a church reception. The family was shocked that they were not
even consulted about the use of the parsonage. The response from one of
the deacons was, "The parsonage belongs to the church, not to you."

A youth minister was questioned about whether he was qualified to serve the church in light of the fact that his wife had expressed her opinions in a Bible study with some of the women. He was surprised that his ministry would be called into question and that his wife didn't have the freedom to express herself along with the rest of the women present in the Bible study.

A personnel committee meeting was called to discuss why their church was not being properly cleaned. When the new pastor had arrived, he had not been told that his wife was required to clean the building each week as part of his salary. That was what the former pastor's wife had done, so the church expected his wife to do the same.

Respect the privacy of the minister's family. Love them, accept them, and tell them that they are as important to the church as the minister. When a church loves the minister's family, it honors God.

Recognition

A young preacher attended a church service in a small town to hear a famous evangelist speak. When the pastor and the evangelist came to the platform, the entire congregation stood. When the service was over, the young man asked one of the local deacons why they stood when the pastor and evangelist went to the platform. He said, "When you go into a courtroom, you stand in respect when the judge enters the room. When the president enters a room, the reporters stand in his honor. The people of our church have determined that the man of God who leads us also is deserving of honor."

Recently a pastor who had served for over 30 years was honored by his peers at a leadership conference. Information was shared about the pastor's years of faithful service in the Lord's work. At the end of the presentation, the crowd broke into applause and rose to their feet to cheer. The pastor was overcome with emotion and began to weep openly on the stage at being recognized for his contribution to the work of God's kingdom.

Ministers need recognition just like everyone else. Paul the apostle was aware of the importance of recognition as a form of honor in the life of a leader. He wrote to the church at Philippi: "But I trust in the Lord Jesus to send Timotheus shortly unto you, that I also may be of good comfort, when I know your state. For I have no man likeminded, who will naturally care for your state. . . . But ye know the proof of him, that, as a son with the father, he hath served with me in the gospel. . . . Yet I supposed it necessary to send to you Epaphroditus, my brother, and companion in labour, and fellowsoldier, but your messenger, and he that ministered to my wants. . . . Receive him therefore in the Lord with all gladness; and hold such in reputation: Because for the work of Christ he was nigh unto death, not regarding his life, to supply your lack of service toward me" (Phil. 2:19-20,22,25,29-30).

Paul wrote of his high regard for Timothy and Epaphroditus, complimented both fellow workers, and commended them to the believers in Philippi. We must honor and esteem our leaders with the same honesty and earnestness.

Every church needs to establish ways to recognize milestones in the life of its ministers. Churches can use the yearly anniversary of a minister's service at the church as an occasion to recognize past achievements and honor the leader in the presence of the whole church. Some churches celebrate a staff appreciation day at which time the church says thank you and offers love and appreciation to the staff leaders of the church.

When ministers reach significant milestones in their ministry, the church should determine ways to recognize and celebrate their achievements. Typical milestones are educational advancement, years of service in ministry, books authored, denominational awards, or election to positions of significance. Times of recognition help the church to realize what God is doing in the life of its leaders.

Annually, deacons in some churches host a Christmas banquet for the ministers and their families. The dinner provides an opportunity to recognize and honor all of them. Certificates or other mementos recognizing achievement in the lives of the ministers are presented.

Recognition is an act of honor. When we publicly recognize our leaders and their work, we honor God and His work in our church.

Rewards

One of the best ways to give double honor to our ministers is through rewards. Churches should practice rewarding their ministers. When churches practice rewarding their ministers, they are practicing the giving of double honor.

How are ministers to be rewarded? There are many ways in which that can be done. Deacons and committees given the responsibility for working with staff members usually can recommend to the church ways to reward the faithful work of the ministers. Many people forget that some ministers do not receive bonuses, unlike many of the secular workers in the church. If your minister lives in a church parsonage, he is in reality only renting lodging from the church. As the years go by, the church gains property equity that is paid for by the minister.

Ministers do not obey God's call to ministry in order to make money or to receive rewards. Even so, when a church rewards the ministers whom God has given it, God honors that church.

Here are some categories for rewarding ministers. These can be helpful to deacons or committees to help them establish the practice of honoring ministers.

Salary and Benefits

When Paul penned the words in 1 Timothy 5:17 stating that elders should receive "double honor," it was clear to Timothy and the early church what he meant. Additionally, Paul considered ministers worthy of double pay. As you read his words, you may conclude that the statement is a rhetorical exaggeration to make a point. If we believe in the inspiration of the Scriptures, however, we believe that whatever God wanted said was preserved in them. What the Bible says is truth.

When was the last time your church evaluated the salaries and benefits of your ministers? It may be that the staff salaries and benefits have increased less than the inflation rate, if indeed they have increased at all. Every church must take seriously its responsibility to provide appropriate salaries and benefits for the ministers. Here are some suggestions on how churches might develop a realistic plan for evaluating and improving salary and benefits for their ministers.

1. Every church should do an annual review of the salaries and benefits of the ministers of the church. The performance of ministers is to be evaluated regularly, with remuneration given on a pay-for-performance basis. A salary and benefit review should follow to ensure that none has fallen below the cost of living in the current economy. Benefit needs change and must be evaluated on an individual basis. The church must make a practice of evaluating regularly the benefits that it provides its ministers. As the church grows, so should the salaries and benefits of the ministers. Most of them are not going to feel comfortable talking about their salary and benefits. It is the responsibility of the church to make sure that this is done decently and with respect. The church must remember that the salary and benefits are for the God-called leaders of the church. We should give our best to God and His leaders.

2. Every church should designate a group to monitor the salaries and benefit needs of the ministers of the church. What group or committee will be responsible for doing the systematic review of individual salary and benefit needs? Most church constitutions and bylaws have established the procedures and designated the group given the responsibility for this task. The group should be made up of spiritually mature Christians who take seriously their role in matters concerning the welfare of the ministers.

It is necessary that the chairperson help the committee or group understand how important their work is in relationship to ways in which the church honors their ministers financially. Many financial pressures occur for ministers because the group assigned to deal with their salaries and benefits has been negligent.

and benefits has been negligent.

3. Every church should determine the most honorable way to disclose ministers' salaries and benefits information with the congregation. How would you like to have a group of people publicly discuss your salary and benefits and then take a vote on what you should be paid? That is what happens in many churches. It is interesting to observe who in the church seems to be the most concerned about discussing the information about ministers' salaries and benefits. Heated arguments and disruptions in the church have resulted from such discussions, not to mention public embarrassment to the ministers and their families.

Churches need to find prudent ways in which the salaries and benefits of ministers are disclosed to the congregation. Some churches place all salaries and benefits together in the budget for congregational approval. Provisions then are made for those who want to know the individual remunerations to review them in the church office. This procedure can eliminate a major point of embarrassment for ministers who already feel uncomfortable talking about salary and benefits. The church group charged with responsibility for salaries and benefits should recommend an appropriate procedure for discussing and approving those matters.

4. Every church must determine a process for considering salary and benefit increases annually. Churches have an obligation to their ministers to provide each year a fair and honorable salary and benefits package to compensate them for their work in the ministry. Every effort should be made to increase salaries annually for deserving ministers. The group that works on salary and benefit issues should establish and maintain a consistent method for giving warranted salary increases, with church approval, of course.

There are different personnel needs for individual ministers. Some ministers are young and just starting out, others are in their prime earning years, and still others are preparing to retire. Performance is the fundamental consideration whatever process is used by the responsible committee. Even so, all individual matters also should be taken into consideration. The goal of every church should be to reward its ministers who labor worthily with the best salary and benefits possible for each person. They then are expected to give the best of their time and energy in serving God through the church.

Special Gifts

When a worthy minister marks a significant milestone in ministry, the church can use the occasion to honor that leader. There are several ways in which honor can be shown through the giving of special gifts. When the minister has served for 5 ,10, 15, 20, 25 years, and so on, the church can give some special token of appreciation for faithful service to the church. Plaques, watches, or other special gifts large and small are meaningful to the minister.

Many churches have used some of the following times and ways to honor their ministers with special gifts: Christmas, birthdays, and "love offerings" on occasion to meet special needs. The entire church can participate in honoring the ministers.

Every church should want to honor its ministers annually on their anniversaries in coming to minister at the church. A survey of over 1,400 pastors conducted by the LifeWay Church Leadership Division of LifeWay Christian Resources found that only 20 percent of them were recognized on their anniversary. Churches will benefit from honoring their ministers with special gifts.

Sabbaticals

Ministers who have served a church for long periods of time deserve a rest beyond a vacation. Almost every church should include a plan for providing its ministers with sabbaticals.

A sabbatical is an extended period of time for the purpose of study and renewal. It is provided by the church, with pay, for the minister based on years of service. The time can be used for personal or professional development. A sabbatical is a way in which the church honors its leaders by giving them the most valuable of possessions: creative time.

Some churches have established in their constitutions that ministers qualify for a paid one-month sabbatical after seven consecutive years of service to the church. This has proved to be a wonderful experience for ministers and has lengthened their ministries.

Vacations and Retreats

Churches know that each year it is good to give ministers and their families some well-deserved rest. Annual vacation time is standard. Some churches have used special milestones in a minister's service to send its leader's entire family on a special trip or vacation. Other churches have placed money in the budget to be used for annual ministerial retreats for sharpening the minds and skills of the ministers.

Continuing Education

Churches are only as strong as the ministers who lead them. When churches make an investment in a minister in salary and benefits, they must not overlook the importance of providing time and finances for continuing education.

Most businesses require their employees to undergo continuing education periodically. In the world of public education, teachers are required by law to train and learn regularly to maintain their teacher certification. Placing the same priority on continuing education for ministers will be valuable to churches. Ministers need the opportunity to continue their formal education. Many ministers desire more education but cannot afford it. Churches should establish a plan to set aside money and time for their ministers to participate in continuing education experiences.

The group or committee responsible for recommending to the church financial and other forms of support for the minister can develop a system in cooperation with the minister that guarantees a good return on the investment. A church should not underestimate its contribution to a minister's life and work in kingdom enterprises when it honors him by providing opportunity for continuing education.

Retirement

Thinking about the time when work is over is not easy. One of the greatest responsibilities of a church is to work to assist ministers in good financial retirement planning. The Annuity Board of the Southern Baptist Convention has provided ministers with help in regard to retirement planning for many years. Every church should participate in the Annuity Board's plan to provide retirement planning and funds for ministers. For information, write Annuity Board, P.O. Box 2190, Dallas, Texas, 75221-2190 or call (214) 720-0511.

Many elderly widows of ministers live below the poverty line. For many of them there was not adequate planning or opportunity to establish retirement resources. Today, young ministers have available to them a variety of valuable opportunities to invest in their retirement. The church honors God when it helps its ministers plan for retirement.

If your church is unable or unwilling to honor its ministers appropriately, you can do that as an individual believer. There are both corporate and individual responsibilities in giving double honor to the ministers God has given the church. Mary, Martha, and other women assisted Jesus in His ministry. Many individuals assisted Paul on his missionary journeys. When God gives you a burden for your ministers, don't drop it. Accept it as a calling from God to honor and care for them. Several illustrations will help you to see what you can do to show double honor to a minister.

A young preacher moved his family to a state far from any of his relatives. A man in the church saw that the minister had no money to put down on a house. He gave him the amount needed for the down payment. In addition, he bought furnishings for the house. He did not tell anyone that he did it, but he was led by God to do it. The young minister asked the man why he would do such a thing. The man said that he grew up seeing church people give new preachers a so-called pounding, which is a time that people bring goods and foods for the minister's family. But something troubled him about those poundings. The cans often were dented, and the seals on bottles and boxes were broken. He vowed then that he was always going to give the minister the best, not his leftovers.

Another man and his wife take the ministers and their wives out to dinner once a year. Then, the husband buys a new suit for each minister and the wife buys a dress for each minister's wife. They give special gifts to the children of the ministers. Doing those things is their way of showing double honor to the ministers of the church.

The ministers of another church have access to a beautiful condominium. They can arrange times to take their vacations at the condominium. A family in the church provides them use of the place free of charge.

Some individuals have offered the free use of lake homes and cabins in the mountains to honor the leaders God has given their church. A doctor voluntarily provides free medical services to the ministers of his church to show them honor.

One minister related a story of how a man honored him and his family one Christmas. He said that a man in the church congregation drove over to their house and offered his Christmas gift to the family. It was not something wrapped in bright paper with a big ribbon. It was a thoughtful gift of love demonstrated by his washing all the windows of the minister's house.

Talk to those who serve on the church committees responsible for caring for the ministers. Ask the deacons and other members what can be done to increase the honor currently being shown to the ministers. When we honor God's ministers, we honor God.

The story is told that when Charles Spurgeon, a great English Baptist preacher, died, he was buried as he had requested alongside many of his beloved church officers and members. He wanted a spot where they and he could lie together in death as they had worked together in life. The church took care of all the costs for his burial, and many church members subsequently were buried around their beloved pastor so that they might rise together in the resurrection. This illustrates the kind of honor that should exist between a minister and the people he serves, especially for a lengthy period, as was the case with Spurgeon.

Honoring God-called Ministers

When people in your church respond to the call of God to be ministers, how does your church honor them? Every church should have a method of honoring those whom God calls to be future ministers of His church. Do you know the number and location of the people in your church who have surrendered to full-time ministry positions? It is regrettable that many churches do not have any information about those church members who have responded to God's call through the years. No one knows where they are serving and what God is doing through their ministries.

Here are some ideas that a church can incorporate to show honor to these who recently have surrendered to God's call to leadership and to those who are serving as ministers around the world.

1. *Keep an honor roll of those called to the ministry.* Church members should know the names of those whom God has called to ministry positions over the past years and where they are serving. Church members can write cards of encouragement to them. There most likely are pastors, staff leaders, and missionaries serving around the world who have come from your church. What a tremendous thing it is to honor them with prayer and an encouragement card.

Place the pictures and locations of those from your church serving in ministry positions around the world in a prominent place for the whole church to see. Ask families in the church to adopt one of the persons for prayer and support. It is possible that the next Billy Graham may surrender to the ministry out of your local church. Your own children or grandchildren may surrender to God's leadership call. Is your church ready to support and train them?

2. *Provide guidance on further training opportunities.* Churches should establish a plan for assisting persons called into ministry with their education choices. Experienced ministers can help the newly called individuals with these issues. Training opportunities include giving them ministry opportunities in their local church.

3. *Support those called to ministry.* Does your church pray that God will call out future leaders for the church? Jesus said, "The harvest truly is plenteous, but the labourers are few; Pray ye therefore the Lord of the harvest, that he will send forth labourers into his harvest" (Matt. 9:37-38). Churches should design a regular method of praying for those called to leadership. Additionally, churches should provide scholarship funds to assist those who are attending school to prepare for serving as ministers.

Every church should provide specialized training for those called to the ministry. The Pastor-Staff Leadership Department of LifeWay Christian

Resources has materials available to assist churches in the training and development of called-out leaders. When God calls people to be ministers, He gives their home church a responsibility to help them get started.

Honoring Ministers and Planning for the Future

A 60-year-old pastor was sitting in a denominational worker's office talking about his church. He had served that church faithfully for over 25 years. The church had experienced great times of growth, but the community was now different, and growth had slowed. The pastor was active and working as hard as ever, but he could tell that there was a growing dissatisfaction with his leadership. He knew that there were discussions going on in the church about what to do with the preacher. He was afraid that the church was going to ask him to resign. Thinking that no church would want to call him at his age, he wondered what he should or could do.

The day did come when the church asked him to resign. The reason—the church needed a younger man to lead them. So, the pastor resigned from his church at the age of 60. Regrettably, that church has not grown since the day it asked the pastor to resign. In fact, it has declined. There may be a connection with the way the church treated its long-time pastor and the decline of the church. God will not bless the church that dishonors its ministers.

That story illustrates the importance of churches honoring their ministers by developing honorable succession plans. It is true that God blesses His church, but the church must deal with the needs of the ministers given by God. Every church at one time or another must deal with an aging minister and his personal needs while facing the need for a new leader. Succession planning is one solution. It provides the church with a way to plan for future leaders while honoring the ministers now serving with assurance and security in their ministries.

A church pastor was preparing for retirement. He knew that the church needed to go through the pastoral transition smoothly. He suggested that the church select a search committee when he announced his retirement. He would serve for a year, until the new pastor was in place. Then, when the new pastor came, he would move to other ministry opportunities.

Here is another good report. A church personnel committee met with the minister of music who had served the church faithfully for over 20 years. They asked if he would move to a new position, working with senior adults. The church had just called a new pastor, and he wanted to bring another minister of music to the church. The man was delighted with the plan for his continued ministry, so he accepted the new challenge.

Transitions can be carried out effectively in a church that will preserve the dignity and honor of a minister and give continuity to the work. Every church should develop a strategy for succession to ensure that honor is practiced in regard to each minister.

Succession planning should:

1. Recognize the gifts of all the current ministers of the church.

2. Determine the best place for ministers to use their gifts in the future.

3. Provide for open communication with everyone involved in the transition.

4. Take care not to penalize reassigned ministers with drastic reductions in salary.

5. Be open to the leading of the Holy Spirit in His work with everyone involved.

6. Give adequate time and preparation for transitions to take place.

Giving double honor to its ministers is the responsibility of a church. Honoring ministers includes respect, recognition, and rewards. When honor is given by a church to its ministers, God is honored. Our honor for God is revealed by the degree of our honor for our ministers.

[1]Louis McBurnie, "A Psychiatrist Looks at Troubled Pastors" (*Leadership* Spring 1980), 109, 114.
[2]*New American Commentary,* Vol. 34, 155.
[3]Charles Swindoll, *The Bride: Renewing the Passion for the Church* (Grand Rapids: Zondervan, 1995), 187.
[4]*Emerging Trends,* January 1998, Vol. 21, No. 1, 4
[5]H.B. London Jr., & Neil B. Wiseman, *Pastors at Risk* (Wheaton, Ill.: Victor Books, 1993), 27

Study Guide

1. Review the statistics on ministry conditions (pages 51 and 52 in chapter 4). What are your suggestions for a church to assist ministers in reducing pressures such as the ones revealed in the surveys? _____

_____

_____

2. Identify the four cited gifts God has given the church: _____

_____

3. In your opinion, why is it important for church members to view their ministers as called-by-God?_____

4. According to 1 Timothy 5: 17-19, how should ministers be treated by the church? _____

_____

5. Using the material in chapter four, complete the following.
       Define:
       elder _____
       rule _____

       Write a modern term for elder: _____

       Explain these terms:
       "rule well" _____
       double honor _____

6. Reread the example of the personnel committee member who felt the pastor's salary should be kept low (page 58). How do you think Paul would respond to this person?

_____

_____

7. Name the three essentials of honor when focusing on honoring ministers:
R_____, R_____, R_____

8. What is the difference between expecting high personal standards and expecting perfect humanity of your ministers?_____

_____

9. Give examples of how a church shows respect for its ministers. _____

_____
_____
_____

10. Identify ways a church can recognize its ministers. _____

_____
_____
_____

11. List some categories for rewarding ministers: _____

_____
_____
_____

What Would You Do? Complete a chart that lists each minister in your church and each of the three essential areas for honoring ministers (respect, recognition, rewards). In blue ink identify the ways your church honors each minister. In red ink describe additional actions the church could take in each honoring category .

Chapter 5

Dealing with **Ministers** and Church Problems

The deacons knew they had a problem. The pastor had called them together for an "emergency meeting." He said that he needed to share something with them. The meeting began in a rather uncomfortable silence. The pastor then tried to open the meeting. He stumbled through several sentences and finally, with his head bowed, started to weep. When he finally got control of himself, the tearful man apologized to the deacons. He then announced that he had been unfaithful to his wife. The deacons were shocked. No one expected such news. The emotions of the group ran from disbelief to anger. The pastor announced his resignation. The deacons agreed that he needed to do so, but they wanted him to have enough time to make a transition that would take care of his family financially and emotionally and provide time for him to get some help. He agreed.

The deacons met several times and prayed to ask God how they might be redemptive in the unfortunate situation. They worked out an agreement that would provide the pastor with four months of income while he made his transition to a new career, one that would provide for his family financially. The plan was offered with the stipulation that he and his family receive counseling to deal with the issues related to this matter.

Perhaps you have been associated with a church that had to dismiss a minister. No discussion of honoring the minister would be complete without dealing with this difficult subject. Nothing is more quickly reported by the news or gossiped in the streets than a minister's troubles. The personal consequences of dismissal usually are terrible. The reputations of ministers are being destroyed. Some of them are not able to serve any longer in a church ministry because of the damage done by such a situation.

The Dishonor of Forced Termination

A recent survey of 17 Southern Baptist state convention directors of minister relations revealed five primary reasons for the forced termination of ministers.

1. Ministers were terminated over issues of church control.
2. Ministers were terminated for having poor people skills.
3. Ministers were terminated because of the church's resistance to change.
4. Ministers were terminated because of the minister's leadership style.
5. Ministers were terminated because the church had prior unresolved conflicts.

Another survey found these additional reasons why ministers were removed from their leadership roles.

1. Stress within the congregation.
2. Neighborhood churches were growing.
3. Spiritual stagnation within the church.
4. An attitude from society that if you don't win in sports, you fire the coach.
5. The minister could not get along with key people in the church.
6. The minister's manner and presence were offensive.
7. Potpourri—Here a number of excuses were listed:

The powers of the church opposed the minister, staff conflict, the minister had been in the church too long, the church wanted a new face to lead them, the retired pastors didn't support the minister.[1]

The Principle of 1 Timothy 5:19-20

In describing the importance of biblical honor for ministers, Paul the apostle gave insight to the subject of dealing with conflicts. "Against an elder receive not an accusation, but before two or three witnesses. Them that sin rebuke before all, that others also may fear" (1 Tim. 5:19-20).

When conflict occurs between ministers and churches, all should practice the principle of 1 Timothy 5:19. Are there two or three witnesses to any accusation? Because ministers are leaders, it is not uncommon for them to be criticized by others, some of whom are envious. Many ministers have experienced the pain of critical letters, anonymous phone calls, threats, and false accusations. Before any actions are taken against an accused minister, those involved must ask if there is more than one credible witness to the charges.

Under Old Testament law, a man could not be put to death on the testimony of just one witness. It required the testimony of two or three witnesses. "At the mouth of two witnesses, or three witnesses, shall he that is worthy of death be put to death; but at the mouth of one witness he shall not be put to death" (Deut. 17:6). Another portion of the Mosaic law declared, "One witness shall not rise up against a man for any iniquity, or for any sin, in any sin that he sinneth: at the mouth of two witnesses, or at the mouth of three witnesses, shall the matter be established" (Deut. 19:15).

The Practice of Forced Termination

Forced termination is an unknown practice in the New Testament. Nevertheless, forced termination has become a cultural solution for difficult spiritual problems and other conflicts in the church. God's way of handling conflicts calls for rebuke of sin, time for repentance, discipline for unrepentance, and restoration as the final goal. The church must find a way to stop the damage done by the increasing number of forced terminations. It is a non-biblical method of dealing with conflicts. There is a better way.

Determining the cause of conflict in the church is necessary in resolving the problem. The root cause of most conflicts must be recognized as spiritual in nature. Sometimes the spiritual problem is in the life of the minister. Other times the spiritual malady is in the church members. Recognizing the spiritual nature of conflicts is an important first step for the church in dealing with them. Most reasons given for the termination of a minister are symptoms of deeper problems.

The biblical processes of church discipline are to be followed when dealing with the difficult issue of minister and church conflicts. Jesus described the process for confronting these problems in the church in Matthew 18. He identified the steps in resolving conflicts in the church. Whether conflicts are between members or in relationship to the ministers, these seven scriptural steps give guidance for resolving them.

1. *The offended goes to the offender.* "If thy brother shall trespass against thee" (v. 15). The passage clearly reveals that the offended goes to the offender. Jesus continued, "Go and tell him his fault between thee and him alone" (v. 15). The offended goes privately to the offender and confronts him with his fault.

2. *The offender listens and corrects his ways.* "If he shall hear thee, thou hast gained thy brother" (v. 15). The object of this process set forth by Jesus is to restore the relationship between the offender and the

offended. This principle in resolving conflict is found in several other
Scripture passages. James wrote, "Brethren, if any of you do err from the
truth, and one convert him; Let him know, that he which converteth the
sinner from the error of his way, shall save a soul from death, and shall
hide a multitude of sins" (Jas. 5:19-20). Paul wrote, "Brethren, if a man be
overtaken in a fault, ye which are spiritual, restore such an one in the spirit of meekness; considering thyself, lest thou also be tempted" (Gal. 6:1).

The goal of confronting the offender with his offense is to restore him
to fellowship with others in the church. The same steps apply when the
offender is a minister. The church leader is a "brother" in Christ and should
be treated in the same way as any other believer. A private confrontation
may resolve most conflicts in the church before they get out of hand.

3. *If the offender will not listen, take two or three witnesses.* When an
offender is unwilling to hear the complaint against him, then two or
three witnesses should be involved, and the process should be followed
again. The goal is to restore the offending brother, not to condemn or
criticize him. If the offender is a minister, Paul said, "Against an elder
receive not an accusation, but before two or three witnesses" (1 Tim.
5:19). A minister is not to be publicly accused without witnesses who can
establish the truth of the charge against him.

4. *The offender listens and corrects his ways.* The biblical process for
resolving conflict accomplishes its purpose when this step occurs. Even
though Jesus doesn't repeat this statement in Matthew 18, it is implied.
After all, the goal is to restore a sinning brother.

5. *If the offender will not listen, then take it to the church.* "If he neglect
to hear them, tell it unto the church" (v. 17). This is a dynamic and sober-
ing aspect of the process. It means that the "fault" of the offending brother is brought to the attention of the whole church. Most conflicts can be
resolved prior to this step. Paul said, "Them that sin rebuke before all,
that others also may fear" (1 Tim. 5:20). If the offending minister won't
respond to the appeals that have been made privately, then the person
should be rebuked publicly, even if the offense is extreme. A public revelation is a humbling and fearful thing for anyone to face in the church.

6. *The offender listens and corrects his ways.* If the offender repents and
confesses his fault, then restoration has taken place. The process has accomplished its purpose of repentance and restoration.

7. *If the offender will not listen, then treat him like an outsider.* "But if
he neglect to hear the church, let him be unto thee as an heathen man
and a publican" (Matt. 18:17). This is harsh discipline that may be necessary. If so, the offender must henceforth be treated as an outsider. It is at
this point that an offending minister may be removed from his leadership

role. This is to be done only after all the steps to restoration have been carefully followed.

The focus of Matthew 18 is on correcting a sinning fellow church member. Many of the charges used to dismiss ministers are not for sinful actions, but are based on personal conflicts. Termination of a minister is the last resort, not the first, for the church when there is conflict between the minister and a church.

The goal of church correction is restoration, not punishment. Paul encouraged the Corinthians to strive to restore a brother whom they had disciplined: "Sufficient to such a man is this punishment, which was inflicted of many. So that contrariwise ye ought rather to forgive him, and comfort him, lest perhaps such a one should be swallowed up with over-much sorrow. Wherefore I beseech you that ye would confirm your love toward him" (2 Cor. 2:6-8).

When steps are taken to remove a sinning minister, the church's response should be with a view to restoration, not vengeance. Restoration of the believer is the intention Jesus had in mind in regard to the resolution of conflict.

The following questions should be asked when attempting to resolve a conflict between a minister and the church:
1. What is the spiritual nature of the conflict?
2. Are there any credible witnesses to the accusation?
3. Have the principles of Matthew 18 been followed?

If these steps were followed, much of the conflict between minister and church would be diminished or eliminated. These biblical principles are foundational in understanding God's way of handling our conflicts. None of the steps describes the forced removal of the minister as a first step. Rather, the process teaches that repentance and restoration are the goal of resolving conflicts. The process may work best when an outside person (minister or denominational leader) is asked to moderate it.

When these principles have been established as the method of dealing with conflict, minister and church can understand them and agree to follow the biblical process for resolving future conflicts. The entire biblical process and other relevant matters concerning conflict resolution should be set forth in a procedure included in the church's bylaws.

It is to be said that the Timothy passage is clear that a minister who has committed sin and is unresponsive to the steps of Matthew 18 should be rebuked openly in the presence of the church. If he stops his sin and repents, then he is to be restored to Christian fellowship. If he does not stop sinning and repent, then the normal steps of church discipline should be used. The minister should be removed from leadership, and church fellowship should be withdrawn.

Honoring the minister is never to be used as a covering for sin. Nor should it be a method of avoiding the discipline of ministers who are in sin. The truths of Matthew 18 and 1 Timothy 5:19-20 remind us that the discipline of ministers by the church is to be carried out in accordance with the scriptural command to give honor due the position.

_____

[1]Brooks R. Faulkner, *Forced Termination* (Nashville: Broadman Press, 1986), 33-41.

Study Guide

1. According to 1 Timothy 5:19, what is necessary before rebuking an accused minister? _____

2. Summarize God's way of handling conflicts and spiritual problems in the church: _____
_____

3. What is the goal of God's way of handling conflicts?
R _____

4. Read Matthew 18: 15-17. Identify the seven scriptural steps for resolving conflicts:

     1. _____ (v. 15)
     2. _____ (v. 15)
     3. _____ (v. 16)
     4. _____ (implied)
     5. _____ (v. 17)
     6. _____ (implied)
     7. _____ (v. 17)

5. Review the surveys that list the primary reasons for the forced termination of ministers (page 76). Circle the best phrase that categorizes the reasons for termination of ministers: symptom of a spiritual problem or overtly committing acts of sin.

What Would You Do? You receive a phone call from a fellow church member who accuses your pastor of being dishonest. How would you respond to the accusation?

Chapter 6

Selection of New Staff Members

Perhaps no church committee has a greater influence on relations between the church and the minister than the search, or pulpit, committee. This committee is elected by the church to search for new ministers when the need arises.

A variety of ways exist in which churches go about the process of searching for a new pastor and other ministers. Here are some considerations that should be made by the committee that will guarantee that the minister is treated in an honorable way in the process of selection.

1. *Base your search on church needs and expectations* (1 Tim. 3:1-7, Titus 1:5-9). Some committees start with a survey of the church to determine what is wanted in a new minister. The first step should be to review with the church the essential nature of the position and the work and responsibilities of the minister. A committee should never assume that all the members of the church understand the biblical requirements for a minister. A searching church is looking for a minister to lead the church in carrying out its God-given work in the world. This is a process that the entire church should participate in prayerfully.

2. *Treat candidates with respect.* When a minister is being considered, giving respect is a crucial principle. Respect the person's current situation. As the committee deals with the minister, the members should be careful how they deal with the minister in regard to the person's current ministry position. Discussions between the two parties should be confidential. Comparisons should not be made between the ministerial candidate and the currently serving minister or even those who have served the church in the past.

3. *Tell the truth about the current church situation.* The minister needs to understand the current condition of the church. The committee must portray a realistic picture of the blessings and challenges facing the church and how it operates. Nothing is worse than for a minister to come to a

church unaware of any major conflicts facing it.

4. *Protect privacy in the process.* Discussions between the minister and the committee are confidential. Tragic situations have occurred in the lives of ministers when committees have shared information with others in the church regarding issues discussed by the committee. Truthfulness and integrity are the hallmarks of the search process.

5. *Be considerate of special personal and family needs.* No two ministers' families are the same. When a committee begins deliberations with a minister, allow the person an opportunity to share the needs of the family. Treat the minister's wife and family in a respectful way.

6. *Give the entire family adequate opportunities to come and visit the church and community prior to any decision being made.* The family needs time to talk together and consider the situation. Provide information about schools, housing, and other newcomer information that will help the family understand the community. In addition, recognize that while a potential minister may be open to God's leadership and a move, the person must be given time to deal with his feelings.

7. *Discuss salary and benefits with integrity and confidentiality.* Ministers usually feel somewhat awkward discussing finances. The committee must regard all such conversations as confidential. The committee should ask the minister to discuss his current salary and benefits and determine whether those levels are adequate. Salary discussions will help the committee to determine how to provide an appropriate salary and benefits package for the minister.

8. *Don't make the selection process a popularity contest.* After reviewing possible candidates, consider only one at a time. An unfortunate committee action is to allow a potential minister to believe wrongly that he is the only one being considered by the church. When a committee considers more than one candidate at a time, it shows that the group has not prioritized its selection of ministers for consideration. No minister appreciates the feeling of being treated like a contestant in a beauty contest or a horse in a horse race.

9. *Keep the church informed, but use discretion.* Church members should be regularly informed about the progress of the search committee. Discretion should be used in sharing with the church the name or detailed information about the potential minister. The committee has the responsibility to protect the privacy and confidentiality of all of the discussions.

10. *Continue the search committee for a time.* By remaining in existence for six months to a year after a minister is called and comes to serve a church, the involved committee can monitor all promises made and expectations set forth.

Further information on search committees can be found in *Pastor and Staff Search Committee,* compiled by Don Mathis and Donna Gandy. This kit takes you from the beginning point in your search for a pastor or new staff member. The kit includes *The Pastor and Staff Search Committee Guide,* and a computer appendix (on diskette, compatible with Microsoft Word) and text files which include samples of letters to references, release forms, job descriptions, congregational survey, call covenant, interview questions, installation service, and biographical form. It also includes a mini-committee training on audiocassette. Order from *Dated Resources Order Form* or call 1-800-458-2772. (ISBN 0-7673-9120-9).

Study Guide

1. Write a brief summary of each of the following search processes:

Base your search on church needs and expectations _____

_____

_____

_____

Treat candidates with respect _____

_____

_____

_____

Tell the truth about current church situation _____

_____

_____

_____

Protect privacy in the process _____

_____

_____

_____

_____

Be considerate of special personal and family needs_____

_____

_____

_____

Give the entire family adequate opportunities to come and visit the church and community prior to any decision being made _____

_____
_____
_____

Discuss salary and benefits with integrity and confidentiality _____

_____
_____
_____

Don't make the selection process a popularity contest _____

_____
_____
_____

Keep the church informed, but use discretion _____

_____
_____
_____

Continue the search committee for a time _____

_____
_____
_____

2. How would following those guidelines honor both the minister and God? _____

_____
_____
_____

What Would You Do? You have been elected by the church to be the chairman of the search committee that is seeking to find a minister of education.
Write a purpose statement for the search committee.

Chapter 7

God **Honors** the Church that **Honors** Him

A number of church leaders had gathered for a luncheon to discuss the direction for their church. They discussed a number of subjects. Many of the leaders were concerned about the current situation. They wondered what they were doing wrong. Everything seemed to be in place. The organization was right. Adequate resources were available, but something seemed to be missing.

Finally, after much discussion, one of the Senior Adult leaders of the Sunday School said, "I believe that we are missing the blessings and power of God on our work." The words of that man express the feeling of leaders in churches all across the country. We need the blessings of God. We need His power to move beyond routine activities.

When churches honor God, they experience the power and blessings of God. Do you wonder why there seems to be a lack of power in your church or your individual life? God's message to Eli, the high priest, points out the solution—use of the eternal principle of honor: "For them that honor me I will honor, and they that despise me shall be lightly esteemed" (1 Sam. 2:30). When God is not honored by a church, He removes His blessing and power from it.

God's Blessings of Power

When we honor God individually, we receive the blessings and power of God on our lives. God honors us when our lives are committed to the three great principles of honoring Him through lives of discipleship, worship, and stewardship.

James told us: "God resisteth the proud, but giveth grace unto the humble. Submit yourselves therefore to God. Resist the devil, and he will flee from you. Draw nigh to God, and he will draw nigh to you. Cleanse your hands, ye sinners; and purify your hearts, ye double minded. . . . Humble yourselves in the sight of the Lord, and he shall lift you up" (Jas. 4:6-8,10).

If you are a believer who submits to God and draws near to Him in regular worship and fellowship, God's Word promises that He will "lift you up." He will honor you. *Submission to God results in honor from God.* Psalm 112 says: "Blessed is the man that feareth the Lord, that delighteth greatly in his commandments. His seed shall be mighty upon earth: the generation of the upright shall be blessed. Wealth and riches shall be in his house: and his righteousness endureth for ever. . . . A good man sheweth favour, and lendeth: he will guide his affairs with discretion. . . . his heart is fixed, trusting in the Lord. His heart is established, he shall not be afraid, . . . He hath dispersed, he hath given to the poor; his righteousness endureth for ever; his horn shall be exalted with honor" (vv. 1-3; 5,7-9).

Perhaps you have heard the joking statement of some ministers: "I love the church; it's the people I can't stand!" That attitude demonstrates why God intends for us to honor others. Our relationship with others says much about our honor for God. How can we honor others if we do not honor God first? When believers give preference to one another and submit to the authorities whom God has placed over them, they express their honor for God. When churches show double honor for their ministers, they honor God.

In God's grand design He has tied His honor to our relationship with others. You cannot honor God if you do not honor others. The scriptural lessons of submission and obedience are essential life principles in the believer's life. Until we learn those lessons and practice them in our daily experience, we are not living lives that honor God.

A Church that Honored God

God's Word promises that honor will be given to believers as we submit to Him now and also someday in heaven as we stand before the Lord Jesus Christ. Furthermore, God blesses the church corporately as we honor Him. In the Book of Acts, Luke recounted God's blessings on the Jerusalem church, a church that honored God.

Luke began by describing the actions of the church and how it demonstrated the actions of giving honor. The early believers lived lives of committed discipleship. Those were hard days—times of persecution and adversity. It cost people a great deal to follow Jesus Christ as Lord.

Believers in the church at Jerusalem modeled a life of discipleship.

Luke wrote of them: "Then they that gladly received his word were bap-
tized: and the same day there were added unto them about three thousand
souls. And they continued stedfastly in the apostles' doctrine and fellowship, and in breaking of bread, and in prayers. And fear came upon every
soul: and many wonders and signs were done by the apostles. And all that
believed were together, and had all things common; And sold their possessions and goods, and parted them to all men, as every man had need. And
they, continuing daily with one accord in the temple, and breaking bread
from house to house, did eat their meat with gladness and singleness of
heart, Praising God, and having favour with all the people. And the Lord
added to the church daily such as should be saved" (Acts 2:41-47).

The church was honored by God in relationship to people. The
believers had favor with other people. They recognized that there was
something different about the believers, so they honored them. The people may not have accepted what was said, but they still favored the believers. Does your church have favor with the people in your community?
God blesses the faithful church with the favor of others.

In addition, the Jerusalem church experienced the honor of God's
power. The church was in "one accord." People were being saved. Lives
were being changed. The ministers were preaching with power. All of
those actions are marks of the blessings of God. God honors the church
that honors Him.

The Jerusalem church honored the leaders. The ministers of the
church saw the need to spend their time in study and prayer. So, the
church selected what some Bible scholars consider the first deacons, even
though the term is not used in Acts 6, to assist the apostles in meeting the
ministry needs of the church. Luke recorded, "And the word of God
increased; and the number of the disciples multiplied in Jerusalem greatly;
and a great company of the priests were obedient to the faith" (Acts 6:7).

God blessed the church with continued growth. New believers were
added to the Jerusalem church. We don't always make a connection
between church growth and honoring God, but that is what Scripture
teaches. Can it be that many churches today are not experiencing growth
and the other blessings of God because they are dishonoring God in one
or more of the areas that have been pointed out in this writing?

The Jerusalem church stands as a model of a church that honored
God. How does your church match up? When you evaluate the work of
God in your church, does it compare to what you read in the Book of
Acts? You have heard the expression "You can't outgive God." The same
principle is true in relationship to honor. God honors the church that
honors Him. The more we honor God, the more he honors us.

Paul called Timothy to live a life of obedience and honor to God. The same challenge and command is given to us today. When we honor God and the ministers He gives the churches, we will see the hand of God at work. He will honor the church that gives honor.

> *I give thee charge in the sight of God, who quickeneth all things, and before Christ Jesus, who before Pontius Pilate witnessed a good confession; That thou keep this commandment without spot, unrebukeable, until the appearing of our Lord Jesus Christ: Which in his times he shall shew, who is the blessed and only Potentate, the King of kings, and Lord of lords; Who only hath immortality, dwelling in the light which no man can approach unto; whom no man hath seen, nor can see: to whom be honor and power everlasting. Amen. 1 Timothy 6:13-16*

Study Guide

1. Read 1 Samuel 2:30. What is God calling His people to do?_____

_____

What are the consequences that God gives regarding honor? _____

_____

_____

2. Read the verses in Psalm 112 written on page 86. Circle the words that describe the results of fearing and submitting to God.
   How would you describe God's response to the man who honors Him?_____

3. Explain why you agree or disagree with this statement: "Our relationship with others says much about our honor for God."

_____

_____

4. Underline the phrase, "having favor with all the people" on page 87. What actions of the believers caused them to have favor with the people?

_____

_____

5. How did those actions honor God? _____

_____

6. Describe the relationship your church has with the people in your community. _____

_____

What Would You Do? Evaluate the signs you see at your church that show God returning the honor to your church. Are there steps your church needs to take to become a more honoring body of believers—toward God? toward your church members? toward your ministers? toward the community?

Deacon Ministry Resources and Services

Conferences

- **Associational and State Conferences and Workshops**

Local associations and state conventions offer opportunities for deacon training at various times during the year. These conferences often involve opportunities for training for the spouse of a deacon as well as the deacon. Having these conferences in closer geographical proximity to the churches provides more convenience for a larger number of deacons. It also provides an excellent opportunity for the pastor to attend with his deacons and spouses and so build a closer team relationship. You can learn more about the conferences in your area by calling your local Director of Associational Missions. You can learn about state conferences by calling your state convention office and talking to the person who relates to deacon ministry.

- **National and Regional Conferences**

Each year at Ridgecrest Conference Center in North Carolina and Glorieta Conference Center in New Mexico, a national conference on deacon ministry convenes during the National Conference for Church Leadership. These conferences give the ones attending the opportunity to learn from nationally qualified teachers. They also can fellowship with other deacons from across the Southern Baptist Convention and learn new skills for effective deacon ministry. Conference offerings include choices for deacons and their wives. Additionally, those attending participate in the Bible study and worship times with the entire campus. The conferees may choose from either a weekend package of conferences or a week-long package.

A deacon and spouse can attend a regional conference near their church. The time frame offers a conference geographically closer to an individual church while retaining many of the features of the national conferences.

Your church can find information about any of these conferences by calling the Pastor-Staff Leadership Department at LifeWay Christian Resources of the Southern Baptist Convention at (615) 251-2471 or 251-2052.

Resources

The following print and video resources will help those involved in deacon ministry function more effectively. Order these resources from your local LifeWay Christian Store (formerly Baptist Book Store) or by calling 1-800-458-2772 at LifeWay Christian Resources.

• *The Ministry of Baptist Deacons* by Robert Sheffield, ISBN 0763-1944-3

This book provides the basic understandings of deacon ministry. It focuses on the biblical role of deacons; the election of qualified deacon ministers; the deacon ministries of leadership; proclaiming and caregiving; organizing for ministry; and growing as a deacon minister.

• *The Deacon.* This quarterly magazine offers practical suggestions that enable deacons to learn more about their ministry role in your church and community. It will help deacons carry out their deacon ministry responsibilities from visitation to dealing with church conflicts. You will also find inspirational devotions for your deacons meetings and training suggestions. Order the magazine from your *Dated Resources Order Form.*

• *Deacons:Partners in Ministry and Growth* Kit by Jim Henry, ISBN 0763-3897-9

This six-lesson deacon training resource teaches deacons to become partners together with your church staff in ministering to church members and guests, and in promoting church growth.

The contents of the kit include six 25-minute lessons on videotape; 12 videotape 5-7 minute "micro messages;" interactive workbook; facilitator's guide; audiocassette kit; and instruction guide, among other items.

• *Deacons as Leaders* compiled by Robert Sheffield, ISBN 07673 1956 7

One of the key roles for deacons in the church involves leadership. In this book a deacon will learn the biblical leadership model for church and community ministry, how to serve as a change agent, the proper role of deacons when churches undergo times of transition, and how to work as a team with the pastor and staff.

• *Deacon Ministry Planning Guide,* Revised by Robert Sheffield, ISBN 0763-1950-8

This resource enables deacons to plan for and carry out their ministry in the local church in an effective, consistent manner. It contains material on a planning process, different deacon ministry plans, how to plan a deacons retreat, and how to plan training for deacons.

- *Equipping Deacons to Confront Conflict* compiled by James E. White and Robert Sheffield, ISBN 07673-1949-4

This book enables pastors and deacons to learn the basics about conflict and conflict management. Through this knowledge, they can take positive actions in times of church conflict by identifying the real issues, negotiating creatively, and leading toward a constructive resolution.

- *Equipping Deacons in Caring Skills* by Homer Carter, ISBN 07673-2056-5

Through the study of this resource, deacons will improve skills such as building trust, listening, determining needs, improving communication, finding solutions, referring, and following up. Relates to various needs: guilt, grief, doubt, marriage, separation, depression, addiction, conflict, retirement, loneliness.

- *Equipping Deacons in Caring Skills,* V.2 compiled by Robert Sheffield, ISBN 07673-1943-5

This training tool builds on the material found in the above mentioned resource. It gives help in recognizing and providing practical care in crisis situations, including physical and child abuse, divorce, unusual deaths, caring for handicapped children, financial stress, and others.

- *Help! I'm a Deacon's Wife* ISBN 07673-2961-1

This book provides material written by women for women serving as deacons' wives. Readers find suggestions on managing limited time, maintaining a healthy marriage, growing spiritually, and carrying out practical ministry with their deacon husbands.

Teaching Strategies

These teaching ideas are designed to help you teach Dr. Miller's book, *Honoring the Ministry*. Included are discussion questions, visual ideas, and case studies to use for application. The teaching plan is organized into five, 60-90 minute sessions. Each session suggests ways to set up learning readiness, involve the learners, and apply the principles.

Distribute the book before the sessions begin. Ask participants to read the Introduction and the first two chapters and complete the study questions after each chapter before session one.

Session One: Studying Honor
    Material to be reviewed: Introduction, Chapters 1 and 2.
    Suggested Visuals: Use for Power Point on the computer, overhead
            projector, or poster:

1. Biblical Principles of Honor
   - All honor belongs to Jesus Christ.
   - God honors those who honor Him.
   - When we surrender to the lordship of Jesus Christ, we honor God.
   - When we worship in spirit and truth, we honor God.
   - When we give our possessions to God, we honor God.
   - When we honor each other, we honor God.
   - When we submit to authorities, we honor God.
   - When we give double honor to a minister, we honor God.

2. How We Can Give Honor to God
   - We honor God through discipleship
   - We honor God through worship
   - We honor God through stewardship

Teaching Plan:
    1. As participants arrive, distribute index cards to each one. Direct them to write a definition for honor on one side, and on the other side list those whom they think should receive honor. (Have these directions written on the chalkboard.) During this time take care of administrative duties.

    2. Introduce the purpose of the book: "To provide the church with understanding of the biblical principles of honor." Briefly summarize the

main points in the introduction of the book. Ask volunteers to share their definitions of honor. Record these on a large sheet of paper or poster board that is displayed on the focal wall (you will refer to these during the following sessions).

Call on several volunteers to identify those who should receive honor. Record answers on the chalkboard. Ask, "How does this list compare to those who in actuality receive honor from the world today?"

3. Write out the seven misconceptions about honor in the church (page 9, Chapter 1) on seven strips of paper. Divide the participants into seven response groups. Give each group one misconception. Direct each group to: 1) decide why this is a misconception according to Scripture and 2) present any evidence that your church might hold this misconception. Allow the groups to work for eight minutes, and then call on them to share responses.

4. Discuss the concept of honor in both the Old and New Testaments. Call on volunteers to use their study guide answers to describe the individuals honored in the Old and New Testaments.

5. Use a visual to review the "Biblical Principles of Honor."

6. Using the material about Eli and his sons in Chapter 2, summarize God's eternal principle of honor. Call on volunteers to identify ways that believers today follow in the steps of Eli and his sons.

7. Point out the visual, "How We Can Honor God." Explain that study groups will look at the ways believers honor God. Divide the participants into three groups: Group 1 - Discipleship, Group 2 - Worship, and Group 3 - Stewardship. Have each group present a brief summary of how God is honored through the assigned principle. Allow groups to work for 10 minutes. Call on each group to share presentation.

8. Divide the participants into small discussion groups. Ask each group to decide how this question from God, "Where Is My Honor?" would be answered by individuals in the group, their church, the world. Allow 10 minutes for groups to work.

Ask several volunteers to summarize the possible responses to the question, "Where Is My Honor?"

9. Assignment for next session: Read Chapter 3 and complete study questions. Close in prayer, asking God to guide your church in evaluating and applying the biblical principles of honor.

Session Two: Honoring Others
    Material to be reviewed: Chapter 3 - Honoring Others
    Suggested Visuals (Power Point, overhead cels, or posters)

1. Honor: recognizing others as more significant than yourself
    Jesus' example: Philippians 2:5-8
    "Let this mind be in you, which was also in Christ Jesus: Who, being in the form of God, thought it not robbery to be equal with God: But made himself of no reputation, and took upon him the form of a servant, and was made in the likeness of men: And being found in fashion as a man, he humbled himself, and became obedient unto the death, even the death of the cross."
    Jesus' Teaching: Luke 14:11
    "For whosoever exalteth himself shall be abased; and he that humbleth himself shall be exalted."

Teaching Plan:

1. Display the visual on honor. As participants arrive, ask them to find a partner and discuss ways believers can honor others in their daily lives.

2. Call on several volunteers to share responses. Briefly summarize the concept of submission and humility as the beginning of honoring others.

3. Divide the participants into discussion groups, and assign each group one of the following case studies. Each group is to decide the biblical way to honor God in the situation and to answer the questions listed with their case study.

Case Study 1: Mary and Ben have two daughters. One is a single mother with two preschoolers, the other daughter attends junior college and is living at home. Mary and Ben both have elderly parents who live in a town about 45 minutes away. Both sets of parents ask to see the couple more often, but Mary keeps telling them that she has to help the daughters with their busy schedules. She found herself telling her mother, "I can't be everything to everybody." Read Mark 7:9-13. In light of Jesus' teaching to the Pharisees, what would be the best way for Mary and Ben to honor their parents? In what ways do adults dishonor their parents today?

Case Study 2: The ministerial staff of the church has presented a plan to change the worship and Sunday School schedules in order to reach more people. A significant number of adults are against having more than one Sunday School or worship service. One member has called several families to encourage them to "stand up to the preacher and his boys," and tell them they are not going to give up being with their friends on Sunday morning. "This is our church," one of the women told her Sunday School class. Read Hebrews 13:17. In light of this teaching, what would be the best way to honor God in this situation? Is it dishonoring to God to rebel against the God-called ministers of the church?

Case Study 3: Jim is a Christian businessman and a lay leader in his church. However, he strongly disagrees with the government rulings concerning salary, insurance, and other required benefits for employees of small businesses. He hires a crew of workers "under the table" and just pays a flat cash salary. Read 1 Peter 2:13-15. In light of this Scripture, is Jim's behavior dishonoring to God? In what other ways do adults rebel against government authority in their lives?

4. Ask participants to turn to pages 44 and 45, Chapter 3, and review the suggestions for honoring others in the church and different groups to honor. Record on a large sheet of paper the ways your church honors people.

5. Divide into work groups. Have each group design an "honoring" plan of action for your church. Allow time for each group to present the plans. Set up an "honor" committee to follow through on this emphasis.

6. Assignment for next session: Read Chapter 4 and complete study questions.

Close in prayer, asking God to lead you into a lifestyle of honoring others.

Session Three: Honoring God's Ministers

Material to be reviewed: Chapter 4

Suggested Visuals (use with Power Point, overhead cels, or posters):

1. Directions for Honoring Ministers

"Let the elders that rule well be counted worthy of double honor, especially they who labour in the word and doctrine. For the scripture saith, Thou shalt not muzzle the ox that treadeth out the corn. And, The labourer is worthy of his reward. Against an elder receive not an accusation, but before two or three witnesses" (1 Tim. 5:17-19).

2. On this visual leave space for recording responses after each
   term.

Essential Elements for Honoring Ministers

* Respect
* Recognition
* Reward

Teaching Plan

1. Write out the first set of survey statistics (pages 51 and 52, Chapter 4) on strips of paper. As participants arrive, hand them one survey statistic to think about. Divide the participants into six response

groups. Each group will answer this question (write it on the chalkboard): If our pastor were feeling this way, what could we do to uplift him?

After a few minutes, call on each group to share their statistic and response.

2. Lecture briefly on the principle of God-called ministers.

3. Display the 1 Timothy 5:17-19 visual and read the Scripture aloud. Call on volunteers to define these terms: elder, rule well, and double honor.

4. Display the second visual (Respect, Recognition, and Rewards). State that these are the essentials for showing honor to ministers. Divide the participants into three work groups. Each group will recap the material explaining the essential honor element and evaluate your church's action regarding this element. The division of the study groups is:

- Respecting the call to the office of minister to honor God
- Respecting the humanity of the ministers to honor God
- Respecting the ministers' family to honor God

Allow time for the groups to discuss, then call on each group to report findings. Record the church evaluations on the visual.

5. Discuss the principle of recognition. Display a large sheet of paper on the focal wall. Using a black marker, list the ways your church recognizes its ministers. Using a red marker, add to the list new ideas for ways to recognize the ministers.

6. Ask, "What is the difference between recognizing the worth of our ministers and giving rewards for work well done?" Briefly review the categories suggested in the book for rewarding ministers.

Divide into work groups. Each group is to compile a list of ways to reward the ministers in your church. After a few minutes, direct the groups to turn in the lists which will be forwarded to those responsible for working with the church staff.

7. Distribute an index card to each participant. Direct the participants to write on one side of the card their personal commitment about honoring the ministers. On the other side of the card, direct them to identify one action to personally take to show either respect, recognition, or reward to each of your church's ministers.

8. Assignment for next session: Read Chapters 5-7 and complete study questions. Close in prayer, thanking God for each of your church's ministers.

Session Four: Dealing Honorably with Church Problems

Material to be reviewed: Chapters 5, 6, 7

Suggested Visuals:

Seven Scriptural Steps for Resolving Problems (Matt. 18)
1. The offended goes to the offender
2. The offender listens and corrects his ways
3. If the offender will not listen, take two or three witnesses
4. The offender listens and corrects his ways
5. If the offender will not listen, then take it to the church
6. The offender listens and corrects his ways
7. If the offender will not listen, then treat him like an outsider

Key Questions to Ask:
1. What is the spiritual nature of the conflict?
2. Are there any credible witnesses to the accusation?
3. Have the principles of Matthew 18 been followed?

Teaching Plan

1. Arrange the meeting room into four case study groups. As participants arrive, ask them to sit in one of the groups and read the case study. Use the following case studies:

Case Study 1: Pastor Fred continues to ask the church to make changes in order to reach the community. His requests include: marking off guest parking spaces, members sitting toward the middle of the pews to allow guests easier access to seating, young and median adults sitting in the balcony, and providing child care for all church functions. There is a group of lay leaders in the church who want the pastor to leave. Their complaint is, "He doesn't care about the members, just getting more numbers."

Case Study 2: Ken is the minister of youth. His youth program is growing and reaching teens in the community. The church is pleased with the program, but many adults are tired of Ken. He is very aggressive about the needs of the youth ministry. In meetings he tends to criticize any money spent for women's ministry, child care, or adult ministries. He is openly critical of anyone who does not actively support the youth ministry. When confronted about the teens grouping in front of the doors and blocking the way, he said, "If you want a dead church, go to the cemetery."

Case Study 3: The church is growing and reaching young families. Many members are tired of the music program. They want music like the church down the street has. Bob, the minister of music, has been in the church for 18 years. Many feel it is time for him to go someplace else. "We need new blood," is a comment often heard.

Case Study 4: The deacons do not like Pastor Gary's style of leadership. He has been at the church three years and still hasn't learned who is really in charge of the church. The chairman of the deacons was heard saying, "He doesn't realize that this is our church. We were here before he came and we'll be here after he leaves."

1. Direct each case study group to compile a list of ways the church should deal with the assigned situation. Share responses.

2. Display the Matthew 18 visual. Review the steps of solving conflicts biblically.

Ask, "How could taking these steps relieve the stress in the case studies?"

3. Discuss the honorable way to deal with an accusation of committed sin on the part of a minister. Display the "Key Questions" visual. Discuss how asking these questions would help in the case study situations.

4. To reinforce the concept of settling conflicts honorably, ask members to share their responses to the "What Would You Do?" situation in Chapter 5's study questions.

5. Briefly review the principles presented in Chapter 6, "Selection of New Staff Members."

6. To conclude the study of this book, read 1 Samuel 2:30 aloud. Say, "When churches honor God, they experience blessings from God. Direct participants to turn to Acts 2:41-47 and read silently as you read aloud. Ask for volunteers to list ways the church at Jerusalem honored God. Record responses on the board. Ask, "How did God honor that church?" Record responses.

7. Direct participants to evaluate both the life of the church and their own personal life in relationship to the last paragraph in the book:

"Paul called Timothy to live a life of obedience and honor to God. The same challenge and command is given to us today. When we honor God and the ministers He gives the churches, we will see the hand of God at work. He will honor the church that gives honor."

Refer to the first session and the definitions of honor. Ask, "Have any of you changed your definition or understanding of honor?" Call on a few volunteers to share responses. Close with a time of sentence prayers.

Additional Resources for Pastors, Staff, and Leaders

The following resources are available by checking the current Dated Resources Order Form or by calling Customer Service toll free 1-800-458-2772. For consultation and other product information, call 1-888-789-1911.

Magazines and Newsletters

Church Administration - This monthly magazine is like a *Popular Mechanics* for managing your church's ministries.

Christian Media Journal (formerly *Church Media Library*) - This updated quarterly keeps church leaders informed about the latest in establishing, operating and maintaining, improving and enlarging, and using media library resources.

Growing Churches - A professional journal to keep you informed of the latest, most significant developments for achieving balanced church growth.

Let's Worship - A quarterly resource packed with innovative and life-changing worship ideas.

The Minister's Family - This magazine will help ministers strengthen their home and revitalize their ministry.

One Spirit: Women in Church Staff Leadership - The definitive newsletter for every woman in ministry work today.

Proclaim - Sermon helps and illustrations are available in this quarterly journal for biblical preaching.

Pursuit - The ideal outreach and evangelism tool to present to non-Christians during visitation or outreach.

Recreation and Sports Ministry Newsletter - This re-designed newsletter is chock-full of the latest activities that cost little and require a minimum of preparation.

Secretary: FYI - This popular newsletter for church and denominational secretaries features timely information to help keep your office "in the know." It also offers secretaries spiritual encouragement.

Stewardship Journal - This quarterly magazine fills an important need by providing practical, effective, and proven principles and tools for sound biblically based stewardship.

Youth Ministry Update - If you don't have time to keep up with the changing world of teenagers, allow this newsletter to help you do it.

These leadership resources are available by calling 1-800-458-2772. Also check with your local LifeWay Christian Stores.

Building Blocks for Longer Life and Ministry - **Tommy Yessick** This book offers practical steps that can improve your overall well-being and literally extend the life of your ministry. 07673 3436 1

God's Call: The Cornerstone of Effective Ministry - **Neil Knierim and Yvonne Burrage.** This insightful and interactive book, designed for individual or group study, explores what Scripture says about God's call and what that call means today. 07673 3467 1

Evangelism Through the Sunday School: A Journey of FAITH - **Bobby Welch.** The author tells how his church experienced a remarkable moving of God's Spirit when they brought evangelism to the forefront of Sunday School. 07673 3496 5

Kingdom Leadership - **Michael D. Miller.** Written for the pastor and church staff, this book examines the differences between secular business leadership styles in the church and Christ-centered leadership as set forth in Scripture. 08054 9295 X

Kingdom Principles for Church Growth - **Gene Mims.** This dynamic concept, the "1*5*4 Principle," leads to balanced church growth through effective leadership. 07673 1889 7

Outreach Teams That Win: G.R.O.W. - **Jerry Tidwell.** This module contains the book by the same name and other helpful resources to help your church begin an effective outreach ministry. 07673 3465 5

The Pastor and Staff Search Committee - **Don Mathis and Donna Gandy, compilers.** This kit contains a book by the same title and provides the tools your search committee will need. 07673 9120 9

Surviving and Thriving in Today's Ministry - **Don R. Mathis.** This book walks you through the basic steps of building a vibrant ministry that will shine for the Lord. 07673 3452 3

Thine Is the Kingdom: The Reign of God in Today's World - **Gene Mims.** Understand the key biblical aspects of the kingdom of God and what they mean to believers today. 07673 3015 3

Toolbox for Busy Pastors - **Barry Campbell.** Find quick how-to help for the 100 most common tasks in ministry. 07673 9124 1

Deacons can better serve your church with these helpful resources

The Deacon Magazine
This quarterly helps deacons understand and deal with key issues of ministry: conflict in the church, ministering in times of grief, visitation.

The Ministry of Baptist Deacons

"Instruction manual" on how to be a deacon. New deacons should read this to realize the importance of their ministry.
(0-7673-1944-3; $6.95*)

Deacons: Partners in Ministry and Growth
Jim Henry, Senior Minister of First Baptist Church, Orlando, Florida, leads in this six-session training resource to teach deacons to become partners with your church staff in ministering to church members and visitors, and in promoting growth. *(0-7673-3896-0; $189.95*)*

Deacons as Leaders
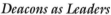
Emphasizes the Biblical leadership responsibility of the deacon – in times of church transition or working with pastors and staff.
(0-7673-1956-7; $6.95*)

Deacon Ministry Planning Guide, Revised

Enables deacons to plan for and carry out their ministry in the church effectively, consistently, and confidently.
(0-7673-1950-8; $7.95*)

Equipping Deacons to Confront Conflict
Instructs both pastors and deacons on how to take positive action in times of church conflict.
(0-7673-1949-4; $11.95*)

Equipping Deacons in Caring Skills, Volume 1

Helps deacons improve caring skills such as building trust, listening, determining needs, improving communication, finding solutions, referring, and follow-up. *(0-7673-2056-5; $10.95*)*

Equipping Deacons in Caring Skills, Volume 2
Prepares deacons to recognize needs and provide practical care in crisis situations, such as abuse, divorce, unusual deaths, handicaps, financial stress, and others.
(0-7673-1943-5; $10.95*)

Help! I'm a Deacon's Wife

Provides much needed guidance, support, and comfort to deacon wives. Answers important questions regarding their roles.
(0-7673-2061-1; 7.95*)

Equip deacons to better serve your church! Call toll-free 1-800-458-2772 (8:00-5:00 CST, M-F). *Email* to *customerservice@lifeway.com* or *fax* to (615) 251-5933. Or use a LifeWay Order Form.

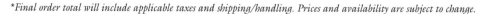

*Final order total will include applicable taxes and shipping/handling. Prices and availability are subject to change.

Notes

Notes